break up!

**WITH
YOUR
RENTAL**

Published by Mindstir Media, LLC
45 Lafayette Rd | Suite 181| North Hampton, NH 03862 | USA
1.800.767.0531 | www.mindstirmedia.com

Printed in the United States of America
ISBN-13: 978-1-7327049-7-8
Library of Congress Control Number: 2018957871

MINDSTIR MEDIA

break up! WITH YOUR RENTAL

BY BROKERAGE OWNER, TV HOST, AND SPEAKER

COURTNEY J.E. POULOS

table of contents

FOREWORD

When I was 23 years old I bought my first home. The price of the property was $50,000, and I put part of the down payment on a credit card. It was a lifestyle altering experience on several levels. At an early age, I suddenly had a lot of responsibility, which turned out to be a blessing. Rather than spending money on things young women like to buy, I was making a mortgage payment.

One of the great things that happened as a result of the purchase is that I became so intrigued with the process of buying a home, I made the decision to get my real estate license, and start a new career.

And while I became busy helping consumers buy and sell homes, I was building an asset by paying off my mortgage.

It all seemed so simple back then in the 1980's.

Very few single women bought homes back then. That number has increased significantly, and in fact The National Association of Realtors tells us in 2017, 18% of all home purchases were made by single females, over twice the percentage as compared to single men.

When I look back at my decision over 30 years ago to become a homeowner, I realize it really shaped my future and was one of the best decisions I could have made.

This is why I am so excited about Courtney's book! *Break Up with Your Rental: The Professional Woman's Guide to Building Wealth Through Real Estate* is a practical guide for today's busy women to stand back, take a breath and plan for the future by investing in an important asset that will build and grow throughout the years.

Today I look back on my years of owning real estate, both income properties and residences and I am thankful I had the courage to take control of my life at an early age.

It is easy to do, Courtney will show you the way!

— **SHERRY CHRIS,** *Chief Executive Officer and President Head Visionary, Better Homes and Gardens Real Estate*

INTRODUCTION

When I was growing up in Central Pennsylvania in the 1980s, money was scarce. My mother, sister, and I lived in a rented townhouse. I remember the feeling of going to my friends' houses, "real houses," and how I envied the safety, the space, the stability of having a *thing to belong to*. I only learned later, after twenty odd jobs and several weird careers, that I was seeing life from the perspective of deficiency. When you feel like something is out of reach it becomes romanticized, and can also become an obsession. Sounds similar to dating, no? But in my view, owning your own home ranks among the better obsessions one can have. It turns out that the perspective of abundance—not deficiency—was the key to understanding the flow, of money, energy, material possessions, and dating.

In retrospect, when I was a child, "home" felt out of reach, but as an adult, there are things I can do to realize that childhood dream. For me, that has come in the form of discovering the power and potential of real estate. Whether you are a creative in this field, like a designer or stager, or an investor just thrilled by the possibility of building an empire, real estate can feed more than just a financial craving—it is inventive, productive, and ultimately triggers that part of us that enjoys the hunt, the conquest, AND the romance.

I was in my late twenties when I discovered the fraud in my thinking all the while I was growing up—I believed owning property was only for married people, and particularly those with kids. I thought that having that house with the white picket fence, SUV in the driveway, and chocolate Labrador was only attainable once I had tried on that glass slipper and it finally fit.

For sure I kept meeting women who waited—waited for the call, waited for the text, waited for the engagement ring, waited to buy any property until they knew for sure that their current partner was a keeper. But it was the outlier badass women I met along the way who showed me what was on the other side of the looking glass. I could actually own a home all by myself, build equity, and leverage it to create some financial independence. I had the good fortune to be mentored by an amazing woman early in my career who taught me everything she knew about real estate, relationships, and thinking outside the box.

I had to unlearn the poverty mentality I was raised with. I taught myself to turn the tables on scarcity and bring on abundance by viewing money spent on real estate not as an expense, but as an investment. It's simple: when you get some extra cash, like a year-end bonus, or your uncle dies and leaves you a bit of money, or even if you just win your Super Bowl kitty, save that money for your first down payment, rather than that weekend trip to Miami with your girlfriends.

With this book, you'll explore the mentality that has been holding you back from growing wealth through real estate. I'll show you why real estate is very much like dating and, actually, how viewing it this way will liberate you from culturally entrenched beliefs you might be holding onto. You will not only overcome all of these mental blocks by the end of this book, you will learn a set of practical and applicable tools for your own journey into the world of real estate, whether you are interested in buying a place to live, rent out, or renovate and sell for a profit. You will also read the stories of numerous women, from a variety of different backgrounds, who have used real estate to improve their lives, give their families and their bank accounts security, and build wealth for both the short- and long-term.

Part 1:

WHY REAL ESTATE
IS LIKE DATING

"It is a comfortable feeling to know that you stand on your own ground. Land is about the only thing that can't fly away."

–Anthony Trollope

CHAPTER 1
LOOKS CAN BE DECEIVING

When I was in my twenties, there were times when I was more concerned about whether I had a date for the weekend, than whether I had gone into overdraft on my checking account. I have always felt like a strong person, but there was still a sense of wanting to please people and meet everyone's needs, even if it was just a guy on a first date. After getting married and divorced, I realized there is a way more interesting, empowering, and lucrative way I could have been spending my time—acquiring property. Real estate.

Real estate is like dating, only far better. Imagine the hunt for Prince/Princess Charming sans crappy one-night stands, catfishing, lies, and the "not ready for commitment" factor. The Multiple Listing Service (or MLS—a large online database of homes for sale) is like Tinder or Bumble, but instead of swiping right for your next potential date or possibly the man of your dreams, you are hunting for a prime investment to build your personal wealth—and this fish wants to be caught! The outcome? You're the one who owns the castle and all the equity that goes along with it.

Real estate listing photos, like online profiles, may make the candidate look younger than he/she is in person, or perhaps all you see are a lazy agent's blurry, finger-in-the-shot iPhone photos, which are probably not at all enticing. But you make an appointment to see it anyway and you fall in love with its potential as your starter apartment purchase or a solid rental unit. When it comes to real estate, looks can be deceiving—a place that appears rough around the edges can prove to be a gem. Whatever condition the place is in, in about three years you're likely to turn a profit and in the meantime you're not wasting money on a rental.

I once knew a woman who was an attorney and spent fifteen years renting. She couldn't make a decision to buy. It turned out her issues with real estate mirrored her issues with dating. She said if she went out on a date with a guy and she didn't like him on the first date, then she would never go out with him again. She was setting herself up for an all-or-nothing scenario. He was either *The One* or he wasn't worth her time. She was actually considering moving to another city to chase a man who had rejected her. Her fear of commitment to her own life and self-worth resulted in her taking a six-month rental and still not buying. She wasn't taking responsibility for her own happiness and security. Think about it, if her rent was $2,500 a month, that's $30,000 a year. That means over the course of fifteen years she threw away $450,000 instead of investing her money in a home and earning a profit.

There are women who say, "I want to be independent and take care of myself," but they don't make the moves that independent people actually make. They work themselves ragged, but only have a 401k and a nice car to show for it. Owning real estate relieves the part of you that yearns to create a home. It means you can stop waiting for a man to provide you with a place to nest. Most women have to have a home. We need design, we need colors, we need baths. We need these things.

When I was growing up in our rented townhouse in State College, Pennsylvania, a home was something I visited, not something I lived in. My friends lived in single-family detached houses with their two-parent families and I loved escaping to that security after school and on weekends, as much as they would have me. My friend's mother Dawn, put up with a lot of my shenanigans as I had a larger-than-life presence, even as a teenager. They still tell the story about the time I dropped spaghetti in the middle of the kitchen floor and it somehow managed to land on the ceiling as well. I was a 1980s latchkey kid. I pined for the lives of my friends where they encountered things like rules and boundaries—they had someone to yell at them to get their homework done or be home by 6 p.m. every day.

My parents divorced when I was very young and my sister and I lived with my mother who worked from 8 a.m. until 8 p.m. every day. My father, who lived in New Jersey, had a Ph.D. in horticulture and managed a plantscape firm. He was in love with plants, and was uninspired by the pursuit of materialism and the rat race of academia, and so chose a low-paying hands-on position, servicing the plantscape of Trump Tower, Penn Station, among other notable Manhattan buildings. My mother worked as a secretary. Neither of them ever owned their own home. I learned very early on that if I was going to have a better life, education was my only way out, and I desperately wanted that ticket to freedom.

When I was thirteen years old I began taking classes at Penn State, and when I was fifteen I was conditionally accepted into the Mary Baldwin College Program for the Exceptionally Gifted in Staunton, Virginia. I saw this as my ticket out of Central Pennsylvania and into the protection of academia. My mother had other ideas, however. We drove eight hours to the admissions interview only for my mother to inform the admissions counselor that I couldn't be trusted. "All she wants to do is party and hang with Penn State football players." Really, she just didn't want to lose control of me. But I couldn't be stopped. I called my father in New Jersey and told him I was coming to live with him and deferred my entry to the following year.

My father was my hero. I lived with him for eight months, finishing my senior year in New Jersey. One month before I graduated as valedictorian of my class in 1994, my father unexpectedly passed away. By this time, I had been accepted into the University of Maryland at College Park full-time, with a Presidential Scholarship, and that's where I was headed at the age of sixteen. My mother had moved to England with her new boyfriend, so luckily there was no going back, only forward.

As you are starting to see, the essential safety and protection of home never existed for me. Nor was there any guidance from anyone in my family about how to create a home, manage money, or build wealth. As I started my first year of college, I was literally flying by the seat of my pants. I had three jobs and was working during the day and going to classes at night to put myself through school.

By the time I was seventeen, I had a full-time job at a public relations firm, Fenton Communications, in Washington, D.C., I interned in marketing at RAS Records, a reggae label, and served on the executive steering committee of the Capitol Hill Women's Political Caucus, meeting with Congressional staffers in the halls of Congress to discuss women's leadership in politics. At one point, I worked as a waitress at a vegetarian café in College Park. I was also the fashion and entertainment editor for the University Reporter Magazine, serving twenty-plus colleges in the Washington D.C. metropolitan area.

While I was still in school, in November of 1996, the University Reporter job sent me on a press junket to Los Angeles. It was eighty degrees when I landed at LAX. They put me up at the Century City Plaza Hotel and gave me a per diem of $100 a day, which literally felt like a million dollars at the time. I fell in love with the climate, the geography, the excitement, and the glamor—everything that L.A. is about.

That school year I was on the Dean's List at the Philip Merrill College of Journalism and I won a prestigious award — the 1997 Daniel J. Edelman Public Relations Student of the Year award, which had a huge impact on my life. Edelman PR is one of the biggest and most renowned public relations firms in the world. The prize was a month-long internship at any of Edelman's offices in the world, so—having fallen in love with Los Angeles—I chose to do mine there. After the internship was over, I went back to school to finish up the semester but I ended up quitting college. I was exhausted. I had been working so hard at school and my many jobs for so many years that I burned out. I decided to become an actress and moved to L.A. in the spring of 1997.

In no time, I went from a promising soon-to-be college grad to living the struggling actor's life in La-La Land. I had a $650 a month studio apartment in West Hollywood and was living a hand-to-mouth existence. I worked a day job for an Internet start-up and my boss constantly bounced my paychecks. I moonlighted as a waitress at Jerry's Famous Deli. I made my living doing commercial and TV acting gigs, but never seemed to have enough money to pay the bills or even get a bank account. I paid for everything with cashier's checks and I had no health insurance. No matter how hard I worked, I couldn't get ahead.

I know what it feels like to live paycheck to paycheck, for savings to be nothing but a pipe dream, and to have thousands upon thousands of dollars in student debt staring me down from here to eternity. If someone had suggested there was a path to home ownership for me at that stage of my life, I probably would have thrown a drink in their face. Home ownership was for other people. It was maybe, just maybe, something that happened when you eventually got married and then it might involve a white picket fence, or maybe just a railroad apartment with a dingy shared patio.

Around this time, I met James, my then boyfriend, and we decided to move back to D.C. and try our hand at "adulting." I got a proper job as an editor for a federal government subcontractor—the Substance Abuse and Mental Health Services Administration Disaster Technical Assistance Center of the Department of Health and Human Services. I was making $37,000 a year and enduring the nine-to-five life, replete with mandatory one-hour lunch breaks and human resources meetings. I used my free time to finish my college degree at the University of Maryland.

By this point my finances were truly a mess. I had a 500 credit score and couldn't even qualify for financial aid to finish my degree. I needed a way to make some real money.

One of the jobs I'd had back in L.A. was called First-Time Homebuyer Consultant. I answered the phone at a real estate firm during the boom. I basically did customer intake to find out what their credit score was or whether they'd talked to a lender yet. The broker I was working for suggested I get my real estate license, but I completely rejected the idea because I associated house selling with deception, like being a used car salesman. It wasn't until I was working at the technical editing job for the federal government contractor, and facing down what felt like the zombie apocalypse every day at work, that I began to rethink my position on becoming a real estate agent. The final straw was when a supervisor came over to me one day and told me I was "working too efficiently" and that they needed to be able to bill the government for more hours.

Later, when I told that same supervisor that I was quitting to go into real estate, she gave me a $30 Safeway gift card and said, "You're going to need this." It was meant to be insulting and I understood the subtext. I borrowed $200 from my mother, her only contribution to my life since I left home, so I could take real estate salesperson classes. Of course, her gift turned out to be the most valuable contribution ever, as you will learn.

After leaving my secure federal job, I began to scour Craigslist ads for real estate positions. I ended up being a real estate assistant for a woman named Polly Driscoll at Weichert Realtors® in Washington, D.C. She was a sixty-two-year-old grand dame of real estate who had been selling houses for twenty-eight years. She was always dressed impeccably from head to toe in Ralph Lauren. Her life goals included "spend time with my grandchildren" or "go to the spa today." She was an extraordinary influence on my life and taught me the things my own mother never did: how to sit up straight and not slouch in front of my computer, how to be graceful, and most importantly, how to think differently about money—getting me out of the poverty mindset that I'd been raised with.

If you are reading this book, my guess is that you are somewhat like I was in my government job. You make a decent amount of money, probably way more than I did, and you dutifully invest in your company's prescribed 401k plan. You sat through one of those dry, informational meetings about the 401k, where two guys in suits explained the virtues of the various investment options on a flip chart. Or maybe it was just a glossy brochure you took home and glanced through perfunctorily over your late night Chinese take-away. If you are anything like me, it felt like you were being sold either a pyramid scheme or a timeshare in Puerto Rico; but it seemed like an attainable, responsible, and risk-free investment.

Meanwhile, you fight for a $2,000-a-year raise in exchange for the stability of health insurance. And savings? The mention of it garners a nervous chuckle, a shrug, or the panacea of knowing that you are hardly alone in this precarious lifeboat. You are saving the minimum, if at all, and just getting by. You are probably single and if you're really honest with yourself, you are hoping that the mirage of home ownership in the desert will crystallize into reality when *The One* also makes an appearance on the scene.

You probably have not thought seriously about real estate for this very reason. For most of us, we have been cultured to view buying a home as something you do when you get married, or are at least seriously connected with a life partner. You also have probably never talked to a lender, don't know your current credit score, and the idea of putting 20% down on a property is daunting, if not impossible.

But don't feel bad, because you are not alone and there is a way out. We are living in a very confusing era for women because we are now more financially free than we've ever been, but we still have the desire for protection and reassurance that relationships have always provided. We are caught between an ideal of trying to achieve Kardashian style, Sheryl Sandberg swagger, and secretly grappling with the Cinderella myth that is so deeply ingrained in our bones that even the best South American shaman probably couldn't cast it out.

What if I told you there is an entry point into home ownership, or simply put, real estate investment, at any price point? Would you be surprised to learn there are tools out there to help the first-time buyer, like an FHA loan that requires only 3.5% down payment? We're talking less than $10,000. Add up what you spend on a few pairs of Manolo Blahniks, Jimmy Choo's, or a week in Mexico with your girlfriends at a yoga retreat, and you could have the ticket to stabilizing your financial future very much within your reach. We'll talk more about this in detail in the coming chapters.

Here's the news: being financially independent and owning real estate is the new wedding band. And the truth is that owning real estate is going to give you more stability than your potential marriage, not that I'm anti-marriage. Not for a minute. But what I am aiming to re-educate you on is the idea of tying your financial future to someone else's, when in fact, it's really a case of putting the cart before the horse. When you are financially stable and have your ducks in a row, you are that much more attractive to a potential partner. "Be the person you want to attract."

In this book we're going to approach real estate like dating and I'm going to show you how buying a house is not necessarily a lifelong commitment. It might be your first commitment and one of *The Ones* along the way. So if you are making small commitments, if you are shopping for property like you're going on Tinder or Bumble dates and one piques your interest, you might end up in an exclusive relationship with it, or maybe an extended fling and you move on after a year or so. If this sounds flippant, bear with me. I'll walk you through all the steps and tools necessary for you to begin taking charge of your financial future. You will find it's not only fun, but also extremely liberating.

Finally, you won't be waiting defenselessly, even on a subconscious level, for someone to save you, which is the killer for the modern self-sufficient woman. The idea we're bred with is that there's only going to be one man of your dreams and if you don't find *The One*, you're just not going to commit to your own life. But if there's no knight in shining armor, who's going to rescue you from yourself and your loneliness? No sense in putting down roots, right? If you're like I once was, you might be thinking you're just going to float around waiting, meanwhile time is ticking, and you're getting older, and you're still paying rent.

Buying property regardless of your relationship status, is taking a holistic and loving approach to yourself. It's knowing you are already complete and then having the relationship be the icing on the cake—an added plus—as opposed to the missing piece. There is a wonderful TED talk by Tracy McMillan called "The Person You

Really Need to Marry" which is all about this very idea — marrying yourself first. So do you want to date somebody who's a renter, or do you want to date somebody who's a homeowner? The person you are dating, falling for, and having a relationship with is who *you* are in that moment.

If you sit down six of your professional single women friends and have a chat about the men in their lives, you'll notice a few themes. There are the men who want to be in long-term relationships and they are usually the renters who may not be as career oriented as you. At the end of the day, you will feel like you're pulling a dead weight. They're not the guys that you want. The guy that you want has a ranch in Colorado and rides horses all day or is an entrepreneur in Chicago who owns a stake in a bar downtown and has a cabin in the Upper Peninsula. They're the rooted ones, but they probably want a rooted chick also. And when you are rooted you are more self-satisfied, confident, well rounded, and intelligent because you are somebody who has actually taken a thoughtful approach to your finances. But if you turn the mirror on yourself, you have a zillion excuses for why you haven't done it yet. None of us can expect somebody else to be what we're not.

It's time to reconcile the fantasy of the knight in shining armor with the reality that men are not being groomed to be knights in shining armor anymore. This takes some burden off of them and gives us a bit more freedom. It also makes us more responsible for our own lives and this is a good thing. This is what our mothers, grandmothers, and great-grandmothers fought for on our behalf in the twentieth century. Remember the suffragettes who fought for the right to vote and the Women's Movement of the 60s and 70s? We are here because of our sisters.

Even when you think you are already looking out for number one in your financial life, you may be putting all your eggs in one basket—your employer's. What if you vest your entire financial future, location, safety, and security in a company that goes bankrupt or belly up? What if you roll into work one morning to discover that your entire division has been dismantled and you're laid off?

Maybe you have that friend, the one who is waiting for a man to rescue her, even though she won't admit to it. When he comes along, she dumps her job and runs off to Asheville with him to open a raw juice bar. Whatever the scenario, it's still putting your financial future in someone else's hands, whether it's a boyfriend, girlfriend, or employer. This is why we have to step up and take responsibility for our financial lives. I am here to set you free from the idea that you still have to dress up in your fancy dresses and parade yourself around, pretending to be stupider than you are to get the attention of a man so that he can feel like a hero when he saves you.

Think about it: imagine how many products and industries would go bust if women woke up one morning and decided they were happy with their bodies? Botox, fashion magazines, clothing brands, beauty supplies, weight-loss programs—you name it. We have an entire economy based on women's feelings of inadequacy or the idea that we have to fit some standard of beauty in order to catch the man. But who benefits? You have to ask yourself: Who benefits from me not being happy with myself independently, with me vesting my happiness in a relationship or how men see me? Who wins? The guy who takes you home on Friday because you've had two drinks and need some attention.

Owning real estate roots you, not to a place necessarily, but spiritually, metaphorically, and financially. *Even if you don't live in the place that you own*, you are an owner. You have gained an understanding of how systems work. You have a tool with which to diversify your portfolio. If you trust that love will come to you and the kind of man that you want to attract will be in your life, you will have no fear of making smart financial decisions. You will be saying to yourself, "I'm making this smart decision for myself, which means the person that I'm ending up with is also making that smart decision for himself."

You can't imagine how many women who I talk to have been paying extraordinary rents. I ask if they've ever considered buying, and their answer is, "No, no, I'm sure I wouldn't get prequalified." They think it's this big mysterious thing. They haven't even investigated it. They have no idea how much money they would need to put down. They have no idea what the prices are, or what their mortgage payment would be versus the rent that they're paying. They write it off as something that they probably cannot do.

While buying a house may seem like it's as big a commitment as getting married, the reality is that if the house doesn't work out or you decide to move to another city, you still have an investment you can sell—and you don't have to split the profits with anybody. As we all know, when you divorce you split what you brought to the marriage. When you sell a house you take all the profit. It is truly a bigger risk in the long-run to tie your finances to someone else than to take a risk on the housing market.

One of the phrases I hear most often is "I'm afraid I'll be under water," meaning you will owe more than the property is worth because the market dips. This is a completely erroneous concept and I will show you why there is no such thing as being "under water." There is never a bad time to buy real estate, only a bad time to sell. Of course, the market goes through cycles so if it's not a good time to sell, you hold onto the property and rent it out until it is. Meanwhile, the IRS will give you a tax write-off on the business loss you incur should your mortgage outweigh the rental income you receive. We will discuss this in further detail in Chapter 5.

Some women think a wedding band is a status symbol, but owning a house is a real status symbol. Sure, a diamond ring flashes to the world *I'm a wife; someone chose me*. Home ownership says to the world *I have power because I chose myself*. Now, don't get me wrong, I know you can't spoon with a house, cry on its shoulder, or have sex with it every two weeks like you can a spouse, and I am in no way suggesting they are replaceable. I'm just trying to get you to see that investing in you, before anybody else, is the most important step to creating the life of your dreams and attracting the partner of your dreams. When you are seen as someone who is smart with her money, you become ever more desirable because others see that as unattainable.

Let's admit that we have been brainwashed to believe our value comes from outside of ourselves, at least partially. We seek our parents' or boss's approval, we want a socially acceptable look, and want to be respected and adored in our circles, families, and communities. At the very least, owning real estate gives you a bargaining chip in the world. It's a win/win situation. Not only do you rise in others' opinion of you, you accomplish something much greater— liberation from the fairy tale, the realization that you can actually rescue *yourself.* You refuse to be a damsel in distress at the mercy of a landlord who decides he wants his house back in a month's time because he wants to retire and live there or a landlord who won't let you paint the walls the deep burgundy you are dying to paint them (don't do this anyway, burgundy is NOT on trend!) The truth is, owning real estate is empowering from the inside out. It changes you and I'm going to show you how.

But let's go back to my mentor, Polly Driscoll, for a moment. Again, she taught me how to think differently about money. She taught me the difference between a poverty mentality and a wealth mentality. One Valentine's Day, she bought $7,000 worth of cookies for her clients. I thought it was insane at first. We put a newsletter in with the cookies and we sent them out. Shortly after that, four clients called for appointments and she made $100,000 in commissions. She spent money to make money.

Polly taught me that a poverty mentality centers on buying *things* with your money. Nothing wrong with things. We all like nice things and when you work hard, it is nice to treat yourself to something you've wanted for a long time. But a wealth mentality centers on spending money to make money. The mentalities are distinguished not by how much money you have, but how you spend it.

For example, someone who has a poverty mentality downloads the app that tells you where the cheapest gas is and will drive an hour to a gas station that charges a quarter less for a tank of gas. She doesn't realize she's wasted her time, which is worth money, and also burned tons of gas getting to the cheaper station! Or it's the person who buys something she doesn't need with a coupon just because it's on sale. Or it's the person who spends money on lottery tickets every week hoping to hit the jackpot, rather than saving that money towards a down payment on her first house purchase. Another kind of poverty mentality centers on hoarding money and never spending it, which means the person doesn't invest and the value of the money decreases due to inflation. Real estate changes your mind about the value of money.

While I was still working for Polly and learning the ropes she said to me, "Why don't you buy something?" So I hunted around and found a studio co-op for $235,000. I had repaired my credit enough to qualify for an FHA loan with 3.5% down. It was 400 square feet and all mine. I was paying $1,200 a month on my mortgage and started fixing it up. Then my boyfriend became my husband and I sold it to buy a two-bedroom apartment with him. I didn't make much profit but covered my expenses, took advantage of the mortgage interest deduction, paid myself back the mortgage I had paid. Yes, I also painted the walls bright orange—because I could! Eventually we decided to move back to L.A. and the two-bedroom became a rental for us, which we held onto for five years.

There is a well-worn truth about real estate and it's that land never depreciates—unlike that pair of Manolo Blahniks or your Prius. But people still think real estate is daunting. How could you spend $300,000 on a one bedroom, you say? Because you're not paying the full price. The bank is taking the loan and you're buying something that's worth $300k for $30,000, or maybe even less. You're paying 5%, 10%, or 20% of the purchase price, so that is your only risk. The bank is truly taking the bigger risk. Your entry fee to home ownership is that down payment. If you're buying the place as an investment property to rent out, then it will make you whatever your market rent is in your area, plus appreciation, plus tax credit. Show me a 401k that will get you that kind of return.

I'm going to break down and demystify the whole property buying process for you, so whether you're ready to take the leap to buy something now or two to five years from now, you will have a plan of action. You will be able to start asking real questions and getting informed about your finances and what loan programs will work for you. And if you can't buy in the area where you want to live, live in a rental and buy an investment property somewhere else. One thing will lead to another, but if you have nothing, you can't leverage anything.

"Buy land, they're not making it anymore."

–Mark Twain

THE PAST DOES NOT DETERMINE YOUR PRESENT

Just as we have to examine our past relationships so we don't make the same mistakes in future relationships, we also need to explore our outdated ideas on poverty, wealth, and real estate in order to move forward into financial independence. Maybe you always go for that dynamic alpha male over-achiever who is the perfect companion for a spontaneous weekend trip to Miami Beach, but when the newness wears off and the threat of emotional intimacy creeps in, he's on the next plane to Rio for an inexplicably prolonged work gig. Or you keep meeting super nice, sensitive guys who have inevitably *just* come out of a long relationship and "need time." The point is, we all have patterns and ideas about what is possible that can hold us back from what we truly want—healthy relationships, financial security, and independence. Sometimes those things are patterns that need to be broken, they're vestiges of ideas or beliefs that demand a system upgrade.

As I wrote in the last chapter, *you attract who you are at this very moment in time.* Akin to relationships, some of your ideas are of another era and you don't even know it. For example, for many of our parents and grandparents, who may have been Depression-era babies, ideas of "buy and hold" reign supreme. Our grandparents were more likely to have lived in the same house from the time they got married until their kids were grown. My childhood friend Lisa's family has lived in the same house for the past thirty-eight years. It was the home they purchased to raise their family. The only home they owned prior to that was a mobile home, which they still own and rent out today.

There is a phenomenon happening in our culture that we can't deny—the majority of young people between the ages eighteen and thirty-four who own a home has fallen to a thirty-year low. Now more young people are likely to live with their parents than with a spouse or partner. The reasons for this are more complex than Millennials being over-privileged or entitled. The Pew Research Center found myriad factors contribute to young people's decisions to live at home, including lack of success in their field of employment, the cost of living independently, and debt obligations. They report that Millennials are moving out significantly less often than earlier generations of young adults.

For some people, the fear of poverty is real. When you come from a place of scarcity, you see everything from a defensive point of view. It *can* mean worrying about feeding yourself, but there is more to it than that. Sometimes a poverty mindset can mean settling for the job that pays your bills or the partner who serves your needs at the moment. Or it can mean that fundamentally you don't believe it's possible to make more money, have a fulfilling career, or find the ideal relationship. You surrender before you even try. It's like the person who never walks into the fancy store, even just to look, because they feel like they don't belong there.

I was a very driven kid and young adult because I was determined to escape the environment I had been raised in. But there came a point in my adult life when I had to admit to myself that my blind ambition was a response to a lack of security and nurturing. It was a matter of survival for me.

At some point, we all have to re-evaluate why we do the things we do and ask ourselves if the actions and results in our lives are coming from our inner child or *who we are now*. This affects how we treat our career ambitions, our material acquisitions, our relationships, and how we define ourselves as successful.

How much time did you spend in high school, college, or graduate school studying personal finance or how money works? Not much, right? So where do we learn all our financial habits and be-liefs? Most likely from our parents and the environment we grew up in, unless we have already set out to re-educate ourselves on this topic. There are other inherited myths about real estate besides buy and hold (forever), such as "don't own rental property unless you're prepared to fix toilets and deal with lousy tenants." In truth, there are profitable ways to own real estate that don't involve either sce-nario. We'll discuss these in the coming pages.

This book is for people who *have* to work or *want* to work. It's for the people who occupy the middle ground between the Donald Trumps of the world, who probably cannot imagine what it's like to ever *not* afford anything, and the Mama Junes of the world who lived a subsistence lifestyle before she made it on reality TV. Those of us in the middle have money to spend, but are usually spending it in the wrong places. Maybe you're doing fine but you are not fi-nancially liberated and live a paycheck-to-paycheck existence. Your life is punctuated by small victories like an upgraded car or a yearly bonus, rather than a long-term financial plan.

Greta's story makes her an outlier in this book, as she was very directed towards home ownership at a young age. Now in her late thirties, she is married and has two small children. Greta grew up in the San Diego area with her single mother who taught her about IRAs and the magic of compounding interest from a young age. When she was in high school, a dream crystallized for her. "I read this story in the news about a waitress who was earning $30,000 a year and she saved up and bought a place for herself. And I thought, oh, you really don't have to earn a lot of money to own your own home." From that point on, at the age of seventeen, Greta started saving. In her twenties, while her friends were paying high rents in San Diego and going out to eat a lot, she was instead renting a room in an old lady's house, or rooming with a bunch of friends, and never paying more than $600 or $700 in rent per month. She told me, "Whenever I had more money I wouldn't spend more, I would save more."

She graduated from college but was never particularly money

driven in her choice of career, which meant she tried out different careers and changed course at least three times...not the surest path to financial security. When she was working at a health food store in her mid-twenties people would ask her what she was doing there, since she had a college education. She would respond, "I'm figuring stuff out."

Ten years on, she had saved $100,000, way more than enough for an average down payment. She bought a one-bedroom condo on the outskirts of San Diego for roughly $210,000, even though her mother thought the location was bad. It was what she could afford.

She remembers going into work after she bought her place. Her co-workers were astounded that she had been able to afford such a purchase. Greta had her shit together, but no one knew. She had recently changed her mind about becoming a social worker and didn't know what her income was going to be, so she wanted her monthly mortgage payment to be as low as she could make it. She put as much cash as she could into the purchase and only took out a very small mortgage. After two to three years, she sold the one-bedroom for a profit and bought a small single-family house in Glendale. She only had to own the Glendale property for one year before she listed it for $399,000 and sold it for $431,000, that's $55,000 more than its original purchase price.

She traded up for a condo in Santa Monica, bought for $480,000 in 2014, and sold for $560,000 in 2016. Between these years she met her future husband. When they first got married he moved into the condo with her. He had always rented and never owned his own place. In 2016, they sold the place in Santa Monica and relocated back east for a job, trading it for a townhome in northern Virginia, which Greta could now practically buy in cash.

Greta is a great example of someone who put her own financial security first, which put her family in a better starting place than many newlyweds. My assertion is that we are still subscribing to a post-WWII normalcy-era convention—home is a place you buy with your husband, raise your kids for twenty years, live for another ten years, and then sell when you retire to a small condo in Sarasota,

Florida. Nearly every commercial continually paints this reality for us—that home ownership must by nature be a couple's game. And if you aren't married, you should rent.

Consider, however, that you could already own a house by the time you decide to partner up. Then you could liquidate your assets so the first house you buy with your partner is closer to your dream house, not a starter apartment. I'm encouraging you to start thinking of real estate not as the conclusion to a love story, but as the building block to your financial future.

Part of the poverty mindset that many of us contend with follows along these lines: debt is bad, something to feel guilty about, so pay off as much of your debt every month as possible, and save a portion of your salary every month (the *pay yourself first* mantra). It would be safe to say very few people actually do this. A 2017 survey revealed that 57% of Americans have less than $1,000 in their savings account, albeit an improvement from 2016 when the same study found 69% of Americans had less than $1,000 in savings. It would be more useful to delineate between "good credit" and "bad credit" instead of lumping it all together as "debt," but *en masse* we don't. The word "leverage" is probably not even in most people's daily vocabulary. Bad credit makes you poorer, like high-interest credit card debt caused by spending on things you can't afford. Good debt is debt that makes you richer.

Don't get me wrong, I am not knocking saving money, and Greta is the poster child for it. But don't let the fact you might not have saved $100,000 in ten years deter you. There are still ways into the real estate market without a huge pile of cash at your disposal. Not to worry, we will get into this in more detail later in the book.

Banks won't lend you money to invest in the stock market, but they will lend you money, at a very reasonable rate, to buy real estate. This is leverage. You are using a portion of your money, for example 10% or $20,000 as a down payment on a $200,000 house. The bank is taking the majority of the risk. You're putting down 10% and the bank is putting in 90%. Yet, you receive the benefits of appreciation of the property over time. In two or three years, you might sell the property for $230,000, depending on the area you live in, and then you have realized a 10% return on your money each year. Not bad—a higher return than a savings account.

Let's play the devil's advocate here for a minute. What if the market dips and you are "under water" because the price you paid appears to be higher than the current market value. Perhaps you have very little equity in your home—you weren't able to put down a big enough deposit? The obvious option is you keep holding onto the property until you gain more equity and can sell or at least break even on your expenses. I guarantee you that all the people who could afford their mortgages, but freaked out and sold during the crash of 2008 are kicking themselves now. Ten years after the crash, the sales prices in my market, in Los Angeles, were exceeding the highest prices during the boom. And, wonderfully, the buyers have equity. The majority of the offers I see come through are at 10% down payment or more. Real estate moves in a cycle. It is not about when you buy, it's about timing the sale. Why are you scared to wait it out? If you really have to move and can't live in it anymore, rent it out. If you can't rent it for enough money to cover your expenses, the IRS will give you a business loss deduction on the difference.

But let's face it, for most of us, the overblown fear of "being under water" may prevent us from even getting this far. We are consumed by media overload and messages that suggest *investing* in real estate as a *wealth building tool* is best left to the Robert Kiyosakis or the Barbara Corcorans of the world and not for everyday people. I want to get you out of the mindset of consuming on the micro-level and viewing HGTV as an ongoing saga of "other people's lives" and get you to understand that there is almost no price point at which you cannot enter the real estate market and begin to build assets and equity.

Alas, I realize that your brain probably still wants to hold onto reasons to be nervous about your potential investment. But just remember, real estate is not like buying a car. A house or a condo doesn't immediately depreciate by 30% as soon as you drive it off the lot.

The first thing you need to do is to start working with some real numbers. To do that, there are three people you should talk to and in this order: a mortgage lender, your accountant, and a real estate agent. The lender is going to tell you how much you can be approved for under current lending conditions, the accountant is going to tell you what your tax deduction is going to be, and your real estate agent is going to help you find the best place to buy given what you're trying to accomplish.

Perhaps you already see a lot of your peers buying property, but just haven't felt like it was something you could or should do just yet. Maybe you've been window shopping—you've done some online research just to see what's out there. Take it from me—online mortgage calculators are mostly incorrect. Get the real facts from a real lender before you call up your neighborhood broker to ask to see some properties. I repeat, *find out what you can afford*. Most people find out that the mortgage they qualify for is higher than they were expecting. If you find you're at the top of your price point with what you want versus what you can afford, a lender will be able to explain your options—conventional, ARM, FHA203k, or FHA.

Say you need more buying power? Perhaps an adjustable rate mortgage could help you get a lower interest rate. Your monthly carrying costs (your mortgage payment plus property tax, insurance, utilities, etc.) will be lower because the minimum required payment consists only of interest, not principal necessarily. Acquire the property, add some value by upgrading the bathroom or kitchen, and refinance into a conventional loan, taking into account the appreciating market and the value of your improvements. Or perhaps you want to build some renovation costs into your loan? The FHA203K loan could be a perfect option—you close on a property at the contract price plus the cost of the kitchen and bathroom renovations.

Buyer Beware: There is a predictable psychology to first-time home buying and it goes like this: Once you've found out roughly what you can afford, you go back to looking at properties online. All of a sudden what you can afford doesn't look good enough. It's like the attainable nice guy is just too…available, so you're not really that into him. And you start looking beyond your means. There is something slightly mystifying about human nature—many of us don't want what is right in front of us. Just as you might ask, if he's so good why is he still single? You start wondering what must be wrong with this property because you can actually afford it.

By now you've found an agent who understands what you want. But she has to talk you off the ledge when you are finding everything wrong with the place you can afford. Then you start doing inspections, but you want the perfect house and you start to feel like you're being taken for a ride with each and every place you look at. Here is where you need to change your mind about the risk you're actually taking. This is not your forever home. This is a place that will get you on the property ladder and you will probably keep it anywhere from five to seven years on average.

Unlike a guy you might meet who you think is a pretty good overall prospect (if you could just fix a few things about him, then he'd be perfect), a house is something you actually *can* fix. A property can present real, concrete problems that can be attended to by a plumber, electrician, carpenter, or interior decorator. Or just you—rolling up your sleeves and putting some elbow grease into the project of making it a livable home either for you or a prospective tenant.

This should be liberating! Real estate is fixable!

Give yourself permission to change your mind about the real risk you're actually taking. Buying property is actually a very safe investment compared to a lot of other things you could do with your money and time. If you ask people who bought in 1970 and sold in 2000 whether or not they made a significant profit, the answer is yes! The "safety" of your investment is not in the buying; it is in the opportune timing of the selling.

Education removes superstition and fear. When you understand what the real risks are you realize it is probably riskier to jaywalk on a busy, rainy street than to buy real estate. But what are some ways, you might be asking, to begin to assess the risk when you figure out where you want to buy? There are some good rules of thumb, which may sound cliché if you have heard them before, but they continue to be true today. Location, location, location. For example, try to avoid buying next door to a battery plant. No sense in taking the risk and having to be part of a class action suit ten years later when you find out the plant was emitting toxic waste. It's also good to avoid buying on a highway or super busy street. Similarly, buying next to an active train, metro, or subway line that rattles by the house every ten minutes or so, is probably best avoided.

At the end of the day, you are moving money from one bank to another bank—you are not financing a Nigerian money-laundering scheme by having answered a dubious email plea. Buying real estate truly is safer than buying a hugely expensive car or even taking a cruise in the Bahamas. But I understand, for some people, the thought of spending $750,000 on a one-bedroom in a transitional neighborhood in L.A. might induce a panic attack. Remember, you are only committed to 20% of that amount. You can always sell it or rent it if you change your mind. Consider looking in neighborhoods that give you the most for your money. In general, it is safe to follow commercial development, public transit development, grocery stores.

Things we have used as excuses to not take action in our personal lives bleed over to financial lives. You might be living in a state of limbo, feeling like you shouldn't root where you are because who knows, you *might* get a job offer across the country or your current boyfriend *might* decide to move to Denver and you know you would follow him. This kind of alternative-scenario based living hinders us from making commitments to ourselves.

I have a friend, Amanda, who was in fact thinking about the possibility of buying a place. But then, her boyfriend did move to Denver and she followed him there. Shortly after that, her mom got sick and before she knew it, years had passed and she still hadn't bought anything because "life just kept getting in the way." The problem is, to most people, buying property still symbolizes being anchored somewhere, when in fact, all it should really mean is you are investing in your financial livelihood. Amanda could have bought where she was, rented it out, and then moved to Denver.

Instead, she missed out on years of potential growth in the property market as well as thousands of dollars wasted on rent.

You need to be looking at the amount of rent you pay over time as a net loss. For example, if you pay $2,500 a month rent, not uncommon in any major American city, that's $30,000 a year. You rent some place for three years and you've just kissed $90,000 goodbye with no equity or gain to show for it.

Katarina, a professional fundraiser in academia in her early forties, grew up in Sweden where she was not inculcated with the "wait until you're married to buy" myth. Instead, she set out to buy her first place right out of graduate school when she relocated from Boston to Washington, D.C. Fortunately she was able to get help from her parents, and with her down payment she bought a one-bedroom condo for $399,000 at the height of the real-estate boom in D.C. She said there was a point in 2008 where it depreciated about 10%, but then went back up. She lived there for three years, then rented it out, and was able to use her equity in the property to buy a second place, which was closer to a home she really loved and wanted to stay in.

She found a two-bedroom, two-bath condo in Mount Pleasant on the top floor of an old Victorian house that had been renovated, complete with balcony and garage, for $525,000. She had done her research and knew it had potential because it was the last neighborhood in Northwest D.C. that was still a bit undiscovered. Katarina said, "I knew it was a gem and I was competing against other offers. So I put an offer over the asking price because I knew it was a great deal for the neighborhood." She lived there for three years and sold it for $662,000 when she moved across the country to take a new job in San Diego. She sold her other condo in D.C. at the same time, which enabled her to find a house she really loved right away in the suburb of Solana Beach. She paid $590,000 in 2014 for the two-bedroom, two-bathroom townhouse, with a small backyard, tucked away on a quiet cul-de-sac, and not far from the beach. Three years later it is worth at least $800,000.

Maybe you're thinking, well she's just lucky. But luck favors the prepared. Katarina did her research and made savvy decisions about her purchases, which has enabled her to leverage up with each purchase and get more for her money. When I asked her why she didn't just keep renting if she knew there would be moves in her future, she explained, "To me it's important to feel like I have something that is all mine, which gives me a sense of financial stability." She also learned along the way to always trust her gut. While she does not regret her first purchase, she knew it wasn't her forever home because the things that bothered her about it in the beginning were the things that became a nuisance as time went on, like the noisy neighbors who had parties that lasted until 3:00 a.m. every Friday night. Nevertheless, she believes it's impossible to perfectly time your first purchase with the market and it's better to just take the leap and do it.

Some people feel too paralyzed with fear to make their first home purchase. It turns out there is neuroscience behind decision-making that reveals that no matter how logical we think we may be in our decision-making process, we are primarily guided by our emotions. Neuroscientist Antonio Damasio studied people with damage to the part of the brain where emotions arise, which rendered them unable to experience emotion. This made it incredibly difficult for them to make even the simplest of decisions. They could weigh their options logically, but couldn't make the leap to a decision, even if it was something as simple as whether to go for a walk or stay indoors.

Studies also show that in our "Google-ized" world, our problem is not about getting enough information to make better decisions, but getting the right information. Apparently, doctors diagnosing heart attacks err more often when they have too much data to take into account. Stanford professor Baba Shiv found that choices can't be made without feelings and "that emotion is essential for, and fundamental to, making good decisions." Overwhelmingly, research supports the go-with-the-gut approach to making big and weighty decisions, while suggesting that you can rely on rationale when it comes to simple decisions without a lot of factors involved. So if you're wasting time on logically weighing the pros and cons of whether to take the plunge into home ownership, your energy would best be redirected into finding out and exploring what your options really are. Because at the end of the day, *we don't know what we don't know*. Ultimately, if you need consolation because you are stepping outside of a comfort zone, just call someone who has done it. Heck, call me!

Sheena Iyengar writes about the paradox of choice in her book *The Art of Choosing*. Iyengar, a professor at Columbia Business School, became famous for her jam experiment. Researchers set up a table in a supermarket with jam samples. Sometimes there were six to choose from, sometimes twenty-four, and they found that while more people stopped at the table with more samples, fewer ended up making a choice and purchasing jam because there were too many choices. "Having too many options, it seems, made it harder to settle on a single selection." The study would seem to conclude that less choice is better. Iyengar's findings lie, a bit surprisingly, somewhere in between. She suggests that more choice isn't necessarily better, but neither is less. "In practice, people can cope with larger assortments than research on our basic cognitive limitations might suggest. After all, visiting the cereal aisle doesn't usually give shoppers a nervous breakdown." Look at enough properties to understand the power of your dollar in the current market, but stop searching for the Holy Grail!

It is not an understatement to say that we are obsessed with choice in America, which is what makes the above studies so interesting. Dating apps like Tinder, Bumble, Coffee Meets Bagel, and OK Cupid, to name a few, have opened up our world to a plethora of dating choices which at times can seem more like a curse than a blessing.

According to *Fast Company* magazine, too much choice wears us out, makes us unhappy, and often leads us to avoid making a choice altogether. Researcher Barry Schwartz coined the term, "choice overload," to describe the state we end up in when faced with a plethora of options. "As the number of options increases, the costs, in time and effort, of gathering the information needed to make a good choice also increase," writes Schwartz. "The level of certainty people have about their choice decreases. And the anticipation that they will regret their choice increases." Research seems to support that limiting your choices when trying to make important decisions leads to making more thoughtful decisions.

The single women I know have war stories about choices they've made in the past. But these disappointments should not paralyze us at this stage of the game. We need to take financial care of ourselves, or at the very least, have assets we can both bring to the table and walk away with. The real meaning of "pay yourself first" is prioritizing your own well-being and financial health, rather than hoping Prince Charming is going to come along and do it for you. We all know this is a fairytale myth that still feeds our culture, but it's so deep in our bones there are times we may still be subscribing to it, whether we realize it or not.

Lisa and I have been good friends since we were thirteen. I spent so much time at her house during our teenage years that I became a de facto member of her family. When we were in our twenties we were roommates in L.A. before she moved to New York, then eventually back to our hometown of State College, Pennsylvania. She moved for a relationship, but it ended in a break-up. She had always been a renter during her time in L.A. and New York, but finding herself back on home turf and single again, she decided it was finally time to invest in her own financial future and buy a house.

Her goal was to find a house that also had a separate apartment attached to it so she could rent it out. The income from the rental would go towards her monthly mortgage payment. She ended up making an offer on her college roommate's grandparents' house which had been sitting on the market for a while because the décor made you feel like you were trapped in the 1960s, complete with rose-colored carpeting.

The asking price of the house had been $235,000, but the sellers were willing to settle for $203,000 and Lisa got an FHA mortgage, which only required her to put down 3.5% or $7,105. She threw a clearing house party and asked all her friends to come over for beer, food, and wallpaper ripping, among other things. She was able to mobilize a huge amount of help and manpower this way. She spent approximately $9,000 on initial renovations, doing much of it herself and hiring contractors when she could afford to. Since then she has renovated the bathroom and put roughly $15,000 more into the house. The rent from the apartment, which was her first priority for renovations, has helped cover her costs along the way.

Lisa teaches English as a second language and has recently launched a kombucha company that sells to outlets in her area. She jokes that for a while her house became known as the "Therapy House." Two of her friends were also going through a divorce and a break-up, so they moved in with her for a year, helping her to further offset her mortgage. In the five years since she bought the house, she has refinanced it at a lower rate and put enough into it to get rid of her PMI (private mortgage insurance) payment. The house was most recently appraised at $275,000.

I love Lisa's story because it bears out my belief that real estate is a solid investment in any area of the country, not just in L.A., New York, or San Francisco. Lisa did not have a huge deposit saved up after years of living frugally, but she was smart and looked for a house with a small apartment which could provide some income towards paying her mortgage.

In the next chapter we will discuss some more things that might be holding you back from taking the leap to home ownership, and how the game of real estate can turn you from a bystander into the star of your own life.

"A funny thing happens in real estate. When it comes back, it comes back up like gangbusters."

–Barbara Corcoran,
Shark Investor on *ABC's "Shark Tank"*

CHAPTER 3
WHY AREN'T YOU MARRIED YET?

Without a doubt, one of the most annoying and perennial questions we have to contend with when we're single is, "Why aren't you married yet?" Or perhaps it is slung sideways in a less direct, but no less stinging manner, such as "Met any interesting prospects lately?" Either way, the implication is that something is wrong with us or we are unwanted in some way if we are not married yet. Obviously, this couldn't be further from the truth. Since you are reading this book, you must be amazing because you are taking charge of your life! Whether you get married one day or not, either way, you will be richer for having built your life on your own terms.

Everyone has a story that usually involves a signature event, one that after a significant blow, causes us to take hold of our own destiny and future. Sara is a real estate industry executive. Her own journey to self-empowerment within the real estate industry came about abruptly. She was a happily married mother of two children when she lost her husband unexpectedly to cancer. Suddenly she found herself a single mom with two children under the age of five. She also lost her mother to cancer less than five weeks later. Besides her children, she lost the two most important people in her life in the span of about a month, yet somehow she found an inner strength she didn't know she had. There were many days she forced herself to put one foot in front of the other, knowing that she needed to be the pillar of strength for her children. Sara says, "That loss changed so many things in my life, in particular, my perspective on what matters. I truly believe grief gives you the power of perspective. The little things fell away and what was left was a burning fire for life, for my career and, most importantly, for my children."

Through her work in the real estate industry, she met some amazing people, mentors and dynamic leaders, and she heard inspiring stories of tenacity, grit, and overcoming adversity. The limitless potential in the real estate industry helped push her forward. She says, "I might never have arrived at this juncture had I not had the rug pulled out from underneath me."

***

We are going to delve into any lingering concerns that are holding you back from breaking up with your rental. Then, in the next chapter we will get into the more granular details of how to actually make your first purchase.

We are twenty-first century career women who grew up with the inherent belief that we are equal to any man in what we deserve and should expect from life. Nevertheless the Cinderella myth is firmly ingrained in our culture and can inhibit us from truly committing to ourselves independent of our relationships, be they with partners, family, or friends. Research even supports this idea. Columbia University psychologist Geraldine Downey and Carnegie Mellon psychologist Vicki Helgeson have found that "women define themselves so much in relation to others that they don't have a separate identity outside those relationships." While this may sound extreme and more like our mother's generation, young women today still have traces of this mentality.

This vision of ourselves can be exemplified by the way we give our power to others in the form of always seeking what we might call a "second opinion." It is more like asking for unspoken permission from our parents, brother, or trusted uncle before we make a big life move, such as changing jobs or considering a real estate purchase. If you don't have this kind of relationship in your life, then you may have learned to be, as the renowned psychologist Abraham Maslow coined, "independent of the good opinion of others" from an early age, which can certainly be a bonus in some ways.

Perhaps you're saying, "But my rent is so cheap, why would I move?" If you live in a major city in the U.S., you are likely paying at least $1,800 per month all the way up to the crazy-making rents of Manhattan in the range of $3,000-$5,000+ per month. Let's take an average urban rent of $2,300 per month, which could very easily equal or exceed a mortgage payment, multiply by 12 and we can see you are paying $27,600 per year in rent. This is more than the average down payment on a house or apartment. I'm not going to sugarcoat this for you: you are effectively flushing your money down the toilet because, while you get a roof over your head, you are not making your money work for you. You are not building equity and you are not getting tax deductions on your rent.

Renting is like being in a relationship that is tolerable because you're having occasional sex. You can't renovate and you are living at the whim of your landlord who is free to raise your rent every one or two years. I do realize that renting gives you an illusory idea of freedom because you only have to give your landlord one month's notice and then you can move across the country if you want. Elena is a thirty-year-old entrepreneur and social media manager who aligns with this profile and still believes that renting gives her the freedom she needs.

Originally from Eastern Europe, she grew up in New York, and moved to Los Angeles five years ago to start her clothing accessory line. She doesn't like the idea of being tied down to one place and feels she won't stay in L.A. more than a few years, so doesn't want to commit to buying. She also told me, "I would rather spend my discretionary income on travel and other leisure activities than on a mortgage."

For Elena, like a lot of women, buying is also firmly linked in her mind to getting married and raising kids. This is when she feels she will be ready to buy—sometime in the next ten years when she meets *The One*. Elena is a smart, successful Millennial but she is suffering from what I call the What-If Syndrome. What if I fall in love? What if my income changes? What if an earthquake hits southern California? Yes, all those things can happen. Meanwhile, time ticks by and money spent on rent is not making money for you. Elena is also probably less motivated to buy because, according to her, most of her friends feel the same way. She wonders if it's a generational thing, "When my parents were thirty, they were already homeowners." I'm still working on Elena and I haven't given up on her yet!

If I can convince you to spend as much time paying attention to your financial health as you do your physical health, I have succeeded. I know you're all up on the latest paleo, gluten-free, or keto diet, you see your gynecologist once a year, and maybe your therapist once a week, but have you considered your financial health lately? Symptoms of not attending to this incredibly important aspect of your life present as convincing yourself that what you have is enough. In reality, most of us graduate from college and simply tread water financially until we get married, if we do. But everyone needs a regular financial checkup.

Jessica is someone who took a long time to buy the first place because she always felt her rent was so cheap. "I had a rent-controlled apartment that was everything you could want in an apartment—it was a one-bedroom, one-bathroom with four closets, parking, and located in the Hollywood Hills, so I could walk everywhere and had access to nature and hikes 24/7. I never had to get in my car if I didn't want to." Jessica is a freelance TV producer and travels a lot for work and pleasure. Both her wanderlust and her great renting deal made her never want to think seriously about buying a property. In truth, she was hemmed in by her good fortune because her money wasn't working for her at all.

The lightbulb finally went off for Jessica when she realized that buying a property was actually within her reach and gave her so many more options as a way to invest her money. "I wanted something to stand on financially in the future and I felt that I could do that with real estate—if I played my cards right." She admits to having to reframe her ideas about home ownership. She grew up in the Chicago suburbs and moved to L.A. seventeen years ago. Her parents always owned their home—but they've only lived in one home their entire lives—the place where they raised their family and where they will retire. As we discussed in Chapter One, this is typical for older generations, not so much for Generation X and Millennials.

Jessica saved money for a year and started house hunting with her boyfriend, because they decided they were going to buy together. She didn't want to end up in a condo or a cramped one-bedroom, which is all she might have been able to afford in the Hollywood Hills, and even that would have been a stretch. So she expanded her search to include El Sereno, a neighborhood with some properties that hit her target specifications. "I have this thing about wanting to be on a hill. I feel like if you're on a secluded street, rather than a thoroughfare, then you're safer."

Jessica's solution for not wanting to give up her rent-controlled apartment is that she didn't. Even though she and her boyfriend bought an amazing three-bedroom, two-bathroom house with a huge deck, she decided to keep her apartment in Hollywood and rent it out to a friend, "just in case." They paid $560,000 for the house and, as it turns out, it's on a hill and has a great view. They made their decision without even seeing the house in person. Their broker sent them a video of the inside of the house and they made an offer on the spot.

Jessica and her boyfriend are thrilled with their new home, which they paid for with a VA loan because her boyfriend is an ex-Marine. This garnered them not only a low interest rate of 3.5% but they also did not have to make a down payment. Instead, they used the cash they had been saving for improvements on the house, like painting it inside and out, re-doing the deck, and upgrading the kitchen and one of the bathrooms. In the end, they have a $3,200 monthly mortgage payment between them, her share being $1,600, which is only $600 more than she was paying to rent her much smaller Hollywood apartment.

Jessica said she expected to be living a more curtailed lifestyle once she was a homeowner, "but our lifestyle really hasn't changed—we haven't had to be any more frugal than before." Her only wish is that she had bought years ago.

Here's the question you have to ask yourself if you're saving a lot of money on cheap rent: Where is this money going? Are you spending it on shoes and trips to Paris or are you putting it into a fund for your deposit on a house? Your brain is very good at convincing you not to take what you perceive as a risk -- deep down you fear that purchasing a place is overcommitting financially. All that is required is to retrain your brain to look at real estate this way--instead of looking at sales prices, look at actual out-of-pocket costs. The amount you are investing is the amount of your down payment and the expenses needed for upkeep. It is *not* the entire purchase price of the home. Or you may think that buying a place by yourself means you are making a sub-textual commitment to being alone. But in reality, a financially independent woman is far more attractive to a potential Mr. Right than someone living just at her means.

If for some reason you ran into financial difficulties and you were worried you weren't going to make your mortgage payments on time, there are also far more programs available in today's world to help owners hold onto their homes than there are for tenants. If you fall behind on your rent, you run the real and present risk of eviction, but since the real estate bust of 2008, there are myriad loan modification programs available for homeowners. For example, the Obama administration introduced the Home Affordable Modification Plan (HAMP) to help stabilize the housing market. Under this plan, your monthly loan payments are reduced by modifying one or more components of your mortgage.

Anna, a reality TV producer, is another person who went from renting for a long time to finally making the leap to buy. What enabled this to finally happen was a piece of very bad luck that turned out to be good luck. Anna had been living in Manhattan for several years in the late 1990s and had grown tired of renting. She was traveling for work a lot and she found she dreaded coming home to her dark little apartment on E. 26th Street. "I hated coming home from business trips because my apartment was crappier than the hotel rooms I was staying in." This proved motivating for her and she started saving for a down payment.

Around this time, she had also realized she wasn't carrying renters' insurance and thought she should get herself a policy, just in case. Literally two months later, she came home from work to find her apartment had been broken into and she had been cleaned out of all her belongings. Not only had they taken everything of value, like the TV and stereo, "they packed up all my good clothes into one of my giant rolling duffle bags and rolled it right out of the apartment."

Needless to say, she was grateful she had gotten the renters' insurance. Not long after, she received a check for about $10,000 to cover the cost of her losses. She started doing the math and realized she had $20,000, enough for a down payment on a studio in Manhattan, and that her mortgage and maintenance costs would be just about equal what she had been paying in rent. The apartment hunt began. After looking at about a dozen places, she made an offer on an adorable art deco studio on 22nd and Lexington Avenue. She paid $129,000 for it (this was the late 90s!) and Anna remembers the broker telling her there was a one bedroom available down the hall for $169,000. "I remember thinking she was insane — I was stretching myself as it was—but it was a beautiful wraparound apartment with two exposures and later I wished I had gone for it."

She lived happily in the studio for five years and sold it for $350,000. She wasn't sure about staying in the city post-9/11 and decided to pocket her profits and rent for a while. That "while" turned into two years as she looked at one place after another and couldn't find one she felt good enough about committing to. She even kept stats of her ongoing hunt and logged seeing sixty-five apartments in that two-year period. Finally, she started looking in Brooklyn Heights and Cobble Hill to extend her possibilities beyond Manhattan. Her broker called her one day and told her about a top floor loft style apartment with a deck and views of Manhattan. Someone had made an offer that fell through.

Anna admits, "It was not love at first sight. It was a fifth floor walkup and the whole loft area was dingy and needed a facelift." However, she was exhausted from her long search and decided to make an offer. She ended up getting the place for $395,000 in 2005 and she has been there ever since and now loves it. Anna does not have a strong appetite for risk, which is probably what took her so long to get back onto the property ladder. In hindsight, she does wish she'd stretched for the one bedroom on E. 22nd Street back when she made her first purchase, where she could have stayed in longer and probably avoided her renting period. "I operated out of fear a lot. Maybe the cautious approach has helped me overall or maybe it's held me back. But I just thought, get in the door [of the studio] and don't take on any extra risk. It was a pre-war building, plumb and thick, and you didn't hear your neighbors. I loved that place."

Anna anticipates another move for herself within the next few years, probably outside of New York. Given that similar apartments in her co-op have recently sold for $800,000 and above, she knows her profits will set her up well. "This is the nest egg that will take me into my next place, quite possibly without a mortgage."

Liz works as a manager in the music industry and also lived in New York for a long time before moving across the country to Los Angeles. While she lived in New York she never felt like she could afford to buy an apartment there, but she was saving all the time to make a deposit. Once she relocated she began planning and saving even more seriously so she could buy her first place. Being self-employed, it was a bit harder for her to get pre-qualified for a loan and she had to do more tax planning (more on how to do that in the next chapter). I put her in touch with a lender who helped her plan ahead with her tax returns for the purchase.

Finally, after a year, she was ready to begin looking and on the first day I showed her six houses. The last one she looked at felt right. She was approved for a loan on more house than she expected she could afford. She put in an offer and got it for less than the asking price. She ended up buying in Highland Park, a quickly transforming, and popular neighborhood for young professionals in northeast L.A. Liz was saving towards her deposit for years because she always wanted to purchase a place that she could eventually grow into with a husband and kids, even though she wasn't married at the time. The three-bedroom house she found was listed for $600,000 and she got it for $560,000.

She refinanced a year later to get a lower interest rate. Since buying it she has also made several improvements to the foundation of the home, put on a new roof, and installed a swimming pool. It is now worth $300,000 more than what she bought it for. Her boyfriend from New York has moved across the country to live with her, so it has turned out to be the house she is growing into with her prospective family.

The one thing Liz wishes she had done differently was to have started building her credit earlier. Ironically, the fact that she was always good with money and never carried any credit card debt, made it harder for her to earn enough credit to be a "safe risk" for lenders. "Not having this made me wait years, when I could have planned ahead better for my first purchase."

The point of all these stories is to show you that women, like you, have found tremendous agency and power in discovering they could buy a home, whether on their own or with a partner. Long gone are the days when we depended upon men to make these kinds of financial decisions for us. The truth is real estate is power and it turns you from the hunted into the hunter.

STEP ONE

The first step you need to take in your journey to buying your first property is to assess your current mental situation. Ask yourself: Have you dealt with your biggest fears? Have you envisioned your "what if" scenario? For example, is your biggest fear that you might lose your job and be unable to make your monthly mortgage payment? Here are some possible solutions for that scenario: 1) get a roommate to help you pay the mortgage, 2) rent it out on Airbnb or VRBO as a short-term rental while you stay with friends or family, you'll be able to pay your mortgage with money left over while you look for a new job, 3) develop a side hustle—something you might enjoy doing that brings in a little extra money and that could be developed further if you needed to, 4) negotiate the terms of your mortgage repayments with your lender—in some circumstances they will be willing to give you more time to make a payment, or 5) as a last ditch move, sell the property if you can at least make your money back on it. These are just some suggestions to show that you actually will have more flexibility *and* stability as an owner than as a renter. Now, if your head is in the right place, you don't want to waste any more time. You want to start positioning yourself to buy something in the near future. That leads us to the second step.

STEP TWO

Now it's time to assess your financial situation. Ask yourself what your big picture game plan is. Honestly, you don't have to project beyond three to five years because, in truth, no one really can and we're kidding ourselves if we think otherwise. Take a look at how much money you have now, whether you have any major debts, such as credit cards, that you need to focus on paying off first. Discuss this with a lender to find your maximum viability as a borrower.

If something is still holding you back, list out your biggest fears. Then address them either by talking with a trusted friend or putting on your research specs and finding out whether they are really rational or if you're constantly looking at the worst-case scenario of what could go wrong. At the end of the day, you have to choose to either be a glass half full, or a glass half empty person. Studies show that people who identify as the former, statistically feel they have more luck in their lives. Also, when things do go wrong, they are better at reframing the experience as something that's outside of them and therefore could happen to anybody, and they try to learn lessons from the experience, thus they are more successful at rebounding from setbacks.

STEP THREE

Once you've assessed your mental and financial status, the third thing to consider is your location. Are you going to buy something to live in where you already live? Do you need to consider locations further afield due to price? Or, if you have an amazing rent deal you don't want to give up, like Jessica, you could keep renting, buy a home as investment, and rent it out.

Before we move into Part Two and discuss more financial details, I'm guessing another burning question you might have is how to find a trustworthy real estate agent and lender to comprise your home shopping team. The best answer is to get a referral from someone you know or work with, maybe even your neighbor or the person whose conversation about real estate you overheard at the gym. Word of mouth is certainly the first choice. You can also tap into my network of trusted real estate agents through my website, **www.breakupwith yourrental.com**.

Deciding to buy your first property may be full of hiccups and mysteries, but it is a worthwhile road to travel. The journey starts with the process of becoming smart with your money. Let's explore how to choose one of *The Ones*—or your first real estate purchase.

Part 2:

THE GOOD ONES AREN'T ALL TAKEN

"I will forever believe that buying a home is a great investment. Why? Because you can't live in a stock certificate. You can't live in a mutual fund."

−Oprah Winfrey

CHAPTER 4
WHEN TO SWIPE RIGHT

Congratulations. You have gotten this far and decided you're not going to pay your landlord's mortgage anymore. You are realizing there are multiple options for home ownership and it's not necessarily a lifetime commitment. Just like with online dating, the inventory on the market at any given moment is going to determine how far your money will go. You have to realize that there are potentially multiple properties, just as there could be multiple partners who could meet your needs at any one time. While you might not want to marry a particular person—or property—they might meet your needs in the shorter term.

What this boils down to is retraining your brain to a new way of looking at risk, so that you make smart investments. It's very unlikely that your first real estate purchase is going to be your forever home. You may date it for a while, but most people own their first homes for 5 to 7 years. The question to ask yourself now is are you purchasing a home to live in or a home to rent out as an investment? There are slightly different approaches to each scenario. Let's start with the former.

BUYING TO LIVE IN
The first thing you're going to do is talk with a lender, ideally more than one. (You can ask me if you need a referral!) Shop around until you find someone who feels like a good fit; someone who you

can talk with easily. Get prequalified before you do anything else. Now you really know what you can afford and what kinds of properties in what areas you should be looking at. You want to work with someone who is going to understand what you want to accomplish and who speaks your language.

I'm going to give you fair warning: this is the point at which your brain starts to act funny. Whether you've been approved up to $250,000 or up to $750,000, the homes you look at within your price range on the market will all of a sudden seem overpriced. Your brain will look for everything that is wrong with the property. I'm not suggesting you throw all caution to the wind and ignore any real red flags, but for all of us—when we are treading the new waters of a first time real estate purchase, our reptilian brains will work hard to find every reason why each potential investment is a bad idea. Meanwhile, for all these years you probably have not thought twice about the rent you're handing over to your landlord each month.

You need to stop looking for perfection because you are not going to find it in your first house or maybe ever, because at every price point there will be something wrong with every house that is available. You will always be working with the following four tools: price, location, size, and condition. You may have to decide on which of those you are willing to compromise. Already you have more to work with because when you were renting your concerns were only price and location.

I once worked with a couple that was very difficult to please. They were looking for their "forever home." They were eventually prequalified up to $3 million but we didn't know that in the beginning, because there was a lag on their paperwork. We started out looking at homes between $2 - $2.5 million. They were all beautiful homes, as you can imagine. They had pools, stunning architecture, beautiful landscaping, and were fully loaded in every way imaginable. These were homes that most of us only dream about owning. But at every place we saw—and we saw dozens—they hated something. "The closet isn't big enough." "The bathroom isn't big enough." "I hate the countertops." I was losing hope that we'd ever be able to find anything they would be happy with because their standards seemed to be so impossibly high.

Then one day, when my assistant and I were dropping the wife off at her own home, she invited us in. When we entered, my assistant and I nearly fell over. The house was a mess. It was outdated, had a terrible layout, cheap finishings, no yard, and was located in an industrial area. We just couldn't wrap our heads around how this woman hated every beautiful home we showed her, and yet her own home left so much to be desired. What this points to, once again, is that our brain plays tricks on us when we are faced with a very big life-changing financial decision. My client had so much choice she was fearful about making the wrong choice.

Remember, you can swap out those crappy 1990 countertops later. Every time you buy and sell all you need to be asking yourself is "can this place work for me for the next five to seven years?" This makes it a smaller, more manageable decision. Anything could happen in this time frame. Your salary could go up, you might get a dog, get a partner, have kids, move to Hawaii. But at the end of the day, you're deciding not to pay someone else's mortgage any more. Have your real estate agent show you places in the order of importance of the four tools you have to work with. If it's location for you, then start there. If you are not finding joy in your first choice location, peel back into the surrounding neighborhoods a bit farther than you had first anticipated. Oftentimes, you can find deals in adjacent neighborhoods that might not have peaked yet.

Genevieve is a perfect example of someone who did this. She works in the music industry and I helped her buy her first home when she was forty. She had been searching in the L.A. neighborhoods of Highland Park and Eagle Rock, her first choices, but kept getting outbid. Then she considered Glassell Park, just down the road from both neighborhoods, but not as competitive a market yet. There she found a two-bedroom house for $549,000 that had just been flipped, meaning quickly bought, renovated, and put on the market with a brand new kitchen, baths, floors, paint, etc. She knew she couldn't afford a fixer-upper at that time so this was the perfect match for her needs. It was even more square footage than she had been hoping for.

She had been bidding on homes in the more desirable neighborhoods in the $700 - $800,000 range and so she put in an offer for $578,000, because she felt it was still a good deal and the neighborhood would eventually support it as the area was growing in popularity. Her offer was accepted immediately. She secured an 80/10/10 loan, which allowed her to put 10% down without paying mortgage insurance. The other 10% is a second mortgage with a slightly higher interest rate. Several years later the house is now valued at $900,000 and she has a lot of equity. She is planning to refinance soon to eliminate the second loan.

According to Genevieve, it took her seventeen years after moving to Los Angeles to get to the point of realizing she could actually buy her own house. "I was always renting. At first my rent was cheap—$400—but towards the end I was renting a small pool house in back of a large party house filled with a bunch of Millennials and it was $2,100 per month." She said it just didn't occur to her earlier in life that she should be saving towards buying her own place. "You save for clothes, for a trip, to decorate your apartment." Genevieve received bonuses at her job and was able to start saving those towards a down payment. At this point, her five- to seven-year plan is to invest more in her current home, perhaps turn one of the bedrooms into a master suite with a renovation, then at some point, possibly sell it. "They should be teaching that this is doable in schools! It was doable for me. I just don't know why I didn't try to do it sooner."

BUYING AS AN INVESTMENT

Buying a property as an investment is your chance to have a fling. My point is not to minimize the seriousness of your financial investment, but to reassure you that the property doesn't have to be 100% perfect. Get rid of the pressure of feeling like it has to be a long-term investment. This alleviates the intensity of seeking and allows you to relax into the notion that "good enough" might really be okay. Maybe it doesn't cross off every box. You might make money in selling it quickly in a fast-changing market like Los Angeles, or if you're in Indiana, you might make real money in the buying and holding. You might also eventually use it as leverage to buy another investment property or to buy a home for you to live in. Or buy three investment properties and when you sell them do a 1031 exchange, avoiding capital gains tax, and trade up to a larger property.

Property only has to be a positive investment. Like somebody you might meet on Tinder or Bumble or Raya, you might want to sleep with them, but it doesn't mean you want to spend the rest of your life with them. What you do want is a positive cash flow return from your investment. You will be working with the same four tools: price, location, size, and condition. Price and location may trump the other two when looking for your first investment property, but being strategic, buying in transforming neighborhoods will reap a better reward.

Your objective with a rental is to spend the minimum amount necessary to get it rented for a good profit. But you also don't want to skimp on the basic necessities that might otherwise incur costly repairs. If the boiler is fifteen years or older you might want to think about replacing that up front. Or if the electrical wiring or plumbing needs work, do that before you rent it out, or better yet, buy a place where these elements don't need replacing. Your goal is to get cash flow positive as quickly as possible and you should aim to give yourself a buffer of about $500 in rent above your mortgage payment. From this you'll need to deduct costs for repairs, property taxes, and vacancy loss, in case there are any vacant periods during which the property sits empty while you look for a tenant. Unless you are putting down a very large deposit, think of your aim with an investment property as long-term or short-term growth and equity. You can play this one by leveraging it with the market.

In most cities across the country, rental prices continue to go up. But if you find yourself in an area where they are going down and your mortgage costs are not being covered, you could refinance to get your mortgage payment down to a manageable cost. You can also claim the difference in your mortgage cost and what you're getting in rent as a business loss with the IRS. The government allows you to deduct expenses for general maintenance and upkeep of the property, managing the property, and other required rental expenses, such as utilities, repairs, taxes, and travel costs. As a landlady, you are also entitled to deduct the salaries of property managers and maintenance workers, such as carpenters, electricians, plumbers, roofers, gardeners, painters, landscapers, and even architects. Talk to your accountant about this.

In most big cities, there is a rental shortage and the rental market is nearly as competitive as the home buying market.

The other good news is that the traditional approach to rental property—having long-term tenants—does not need to be your only option anymore. With the rise of the sharing economy and the prevalence of Airbnb and VRBO, to name just a couple similar platforms, there has been rapid growth in the short-term rental market, which seems set to continue for the foreseeable future. Zeona McIntyre is a young and very successful "Airbnb entrepreneur" who has secured her own financial freedom by building an Airbnb business. She started small, by simply renting out a room in her own house; however, she quickly saw the potential that the market was offering.

Zeona graduated to leasing a condo, which she rented out as a whole unit on Airbnb while maintaining her own apartment and renting the second bedroom. She learned she made a far greater profit when renting an entire place, which led to the next step of buying her first investment property to use solely as a short-term rental on Airbnb. She managed to scrape together enough money with the help of an investor friend to buy it. Now, several years later, she owns five such properties, plus runs a business that manages other people's Airbnb homes for them. She has also automated her business and hired a property management team so that she is able to work very few hours per month and travels often.

According to a recent study, yearly growth in the vacation rental market has been recorded at a steady rate of 3.6% every year between 2011 and 2016. Projections from a variety of sources predict immense growth within the next two years. Just as the company Xerox eventually became a verb to mean making copies, as in, "I'll just Xerox it," Airbnb has now become so ubiquitous that we use it as a verb: "We're going to Airbnb it in Florida this weekend." What started as an inventory of 3,000 homes for rent in 2009 grew to 2.3 million available rentals in 2016. While there are never guarantees on trends, you can still consider short-term or vacation rentals as another viable option for your investment property. And you never know—this side hustle might turn into more over time if you find you enjoy it and the opportunities it offers you.

If you are buying a property as an investment, you need to weigh the costs of buying a "fixer upper" against buying a property that you can rent out straight away. I am personally a fan of the latter; however, if you have less cash to work with up front for a down payment, you may want to consider a house or apartment that needs minor renovating. Especially, if you want to roll up your sleeves and do as much of the work as you can yourself, contracting out for maybe electrical rewiring or a full kitchen rehab. You might qualify for a FHA203K loan, which allows you to bundle renovation costs into the loan.

Sara and her husband Chad are an example of people for whom this option worked perfectly. They rented a condo in Santa Monica together for five years. When they started their property search they wanted to stay on the Westside of Los Angeles but quickly found they were outbid at every turn by cash buyers who were paying above the asking price on everything they wanted. This led them to widen their search to areas of Mid-City Los Angeles they hadn't considered before. After seeing a place in Jefferson Park that wasn't quite right, we pointed out to them that there was another house across the street that was about to come on the market, but was in dire need of renovation. Sara and her husband were interested right away. Sara says, "We weren't afraid of the work involved."

They made an offer, which was accepted and the plan was to finance the purchase with the FHA203K loan to cover the cost of the renovations. It worked because it didn't require a huge down payment. There are some more stringent terms to these loans as they were required to hire the contractor and detail every aspect of work that was to be done to the house before they were able to close, which took about 60 days, more than twice as long as the usual closing process.

The house was a classic California bungalow with four bedrooms, two bathrooms, 1,500 square feet of space, and good bones. Working with their contractor, Sara and Chad knocked down walls creating an open plan living space, converted the fourth bedroom into extra living space at the back of the house, turned one of the bathrooms into an en suite for the master, gutted the kitchen and bathrooms. An inspection revealed the bathtub was about to fall through the floor—all the subflooring had to be replaced. On top of all this, they created vaulted ceilings in the open living space, completely repainted the interior, added central air, forced heating, a fireplace, and transformed the backyard from a dump into a landscaped yard, along with the front garden.

Sara said the one thing she would have done differently was to budget for things beyond the contractor's scope of work for example, faucets and bathtubs. Also, don't order those too early—even if there is a sale at Home Depot—because you will be stuck looking for a place to store them. Most retailers won't deliver to a building site and building sites are notorious targets for thieves anyway.

Sara and Chad paid $550,000 for the house and put $120,000 into the renovation, bringing their total loan amount to $630,000. They have lived in the house for the past couple of years and, while they love it, they want to start a family so they are looking for a more family oriented neighborhood with really good schools. They listed the house for just under $900,000 and sold it for $1,021,700, and just closed on another fixer upper in a neighborhood that better suits their needs. They both really enjoyed the renovation process, which took four months to complete. "If you have the patience for it, it's a really great way to make money."

When you release yourself from the burden of needing to find *The One*, whether in romance or real estate, you open up to the possibility of seeing things as they really are, not as you may fervently hope they might be. It allows you to stop overthinking things and get out of your own way enough to start making smart investment decisions. So while a condo in Cleveland might not be your first choice to call home sweet home, if the numbers add up and it nets you $700 per month as a rental, you may be on your way to building yourself an investment portfolio that will grow nicely over time. To reiterate what mortgage lender Scott Groves said in the last chapter, single people best build wealth by buying a house, continuing to save money, and then keeping that house as a rental property when they grow out of it and are ready to buy a new place. This approach may be easier outside the biggest cities.

Or maybe you've found a house that checks all your boxes to live in, except you absolutely hate the countertops and laminate flooring in the living room. You need to realize you may not be able to do everything you want to put your stamp on the place right in the beginning. These improvements can happen one at a time gradually, when you have the funds to deal with them or have more equity in the property to draw on, and you can make the renovations using a home equity line of credit. I've also learned to always get three bids (or more) from different contractors, as our imaginations really are inaccurate when it comes to the cost of repairs. New countertops may only be a $1,500 upgrade, for example.

It bears repeating, no house will check every box, just as no partner will be perfect. But we do love the ones with character, no? If only marriage counselors had money-back guarantees. Alas, humans are fallible, as we're meant to be. Do not, by any stretch of the imagination, give up on trying to find a great partner for yourself if that is what you want. Just allow yourself to indulge in the concrete tangibility of a good real estate investment, which comes with guarantees on work performed and an almost certain return on your money over time. Find me someone who bought a house in 1970 and sold it in 2017 and did not make a profit—and that is a time span that includes stock market crashes, bull and bear markets and everything in between. However, your five- to seven-year plan is about a house purchase serving your needs and selling it when it makes sense for you. You don't know if the house will serve your needs in the very long term or not. The point is, don't limit yourself to the idea that it *must work in the long term*. You can hold onto it as a rental and recover through changing market cycles until you can sell for a profit.

If you don't come to grips with the "I want my house to be perfect" syndrome you run the risk of screwing yourself out of a perfectly good relationship, as many of us have done in dating and looking for the perfect partner. The reason our brains ask so many questions is not because we're smart, it's because we're fearful. We're afraid of making a mistake that will cost us money, time and face. No one wants to look bad to their friends, family, and colleagues if they buy a lemon. The way around this is learn to ask the important questions of one or two trusted advisors, like your agent, and to look at the financials, but at the end of the day, train your brain to trust your gut. Fear should be your tail feather, not what you lead with. Successful people not only take calculated risks, but they trust their gut.

Antonio Damasio, the David Dornsife Professor of Neuroscience, Psychology and Philosophy at the University of Southern California, says that when the amygdala part of our brains sends us signals that something doesn't feel right, we should pay attention. And the converse, I say. If your gut says it's right, trust it!

"The more you pay attention to the outcome of trusting your intuition in combination with facts, the better your future decision-making can become." Other research on decision-making and relying more on guts than rational thought finds that it can be more useful in certain situations. Shabnam Mousavi, of the John Hopkins Carey Business School, does ongoing research into the complexity of decision-making based on gut feelings. While the traditional approach to decision-making is based on doing a rational and deliberate cost/benefit analysis, Mousavi suggests an alternative: "Create a decision tree that starts with the fundamental question: 'If the worst case scenario of a proposal were to occur, could you survive?' If not, don't pursue it." Finally, consider asking yourself a version of the question, "Am I moving in the direction of an adventure or running from my fears?"

From my point of view, gut instincts perform better when they are based on actual fact. Some combination of intuition and education (this is why you need a real estate agent) will lead you to more than one possible option. The world is your oyster.

I will remind you of the evergreen psychology of the buyer, which goes like this: Once you've found out roughly what you can afford, you go back to looking at properties online. All of a sudden, what you can afford doesn't look good enough. And you start looking beyond your means. You will likely start wondering what must be wrong with a property because you can actually afford it.

Michelle, who works in digital media at a TV network, was thirty-four when she bought her first condo in 2007, just before the crash of 2008. Originally from San Francisco, she lived in New York for several years before moving to Los Angeles. She wished she could have bought sooner, but living in some of the most expensive real estate markets on the planet, she said there was no way she could have. She found herself extremely stymied by the limitations of rentals. "I would even offer to pay the landlord to make improvements and he wouldn't let me. Not feeling like I had control over my living space was eminently frustrating to me."

She saved for a down payment for years because she knew there was an inherent beauty to owning her own place, aside from being able to choose the color of her walls. "I knew that if I could have my money working for me every month I could get to the point where I could just walk away and even if I sold it for exactly what I bought it for, it was like I got to live free the whole time."

She bought her first condo, a one-bedroom, one-bathroom in Santa Monica, four blocks from the beach, for $531,000. It even had a giant private patio and Michelle described it as a "unicorn" in the neighborhood. It was well over her planned budget of $500,000 but she fell in love with it and endured a bidding war to win it. She put down 15% when she bought it and was able to refinance six years later when she had gained some equity in the property. She secured a second mortgage to help her afford it in the first place, despite her family counseling her against it. With the refinance, she was able to pay off the second mortgage. She admits it was scary but says, "I'm super visceral when I walk into a place. I don't see it as an investment; I see it as a sanctuary. This was going to be my home and why shouldn't it make money for me?"

Michelle lived there for ten years before she began the process of buying her second place. She was looking within a twenty-minute drive of her office which led her to the Highland Park area in northeast L.A. Without selling her Santa Monica house, which she plans to do eventually, she was prequalified for $835,000. She found a craftsman style house built in 1907 that was a four bedroom, two bath, 1,700 square feet, for $805,000. The inside had been completely redone, the foundation needed some work, but with lots of windows and two palm trees in the front yard, she could not be happier with her new home.

Remember again that you are never actually "under water." That only means that it isn't a good time for you to sell and you need to hold on until the market changes again, which it always does. Also, the list price of a house is simply a marketing tool—it is a reflection of what the seller hopes to get for it, or at least the best way to create hype. It is not written in stone. It is also a reflection of the market at that time in that particular neighborhood. When you are working with a good real estate agent, she can help you understand what is a realistic price for a property, how to be the most competitive, and which properties have long-term potential or hidden value. Some are keepers; others are passionate flings. Aren't you getting curious to see what's out there? Let's go shopping!

"Forget about perfection. It doesn't exist."

–Barbara Corcoran,
Shark Investor on *ABC's "Shark Tank"*

CHAPTER 5
FINANCIAL INDEPENDENCE IS SEXY

As I said before, no one in my family owned a home, and I wanted to own one. This has no doubt fueled my love of real estate in all its forms. Fast-forward thirty years. More women are graduating college with advanced degrees and more women are engaging in advanced careers in math and science. Even in real estate, women make up more than 63% of licensed real estate agents, according to the National Association of Realtors®. Most dramatically—and most inspiring for me personally—is that more women are using home, and its invention, as a tool for economic and creative empowerment.

Maybe you've encountered the term "creative financing" when it comes to real estate. What it really means is that there are numerous ways to finance a house whether you want to flip it (renovate and sell it quickly for a profit), rent it, or live in it. This can be an empowering discovery and may lead you to consider many options that you never have before. For example, just a few possibilities include, private investors, hard money lenders, property equity, friends and family, seller financing, options and leases, first-time home buyer programs, 401k borrowing, even credit cards, or renovation loans. In a flipping situation, rehab contractors may cover some of the upfront buying costs in exchange for a share of the profits when you sell. All the stories in this chapter are about women who found creative ways to finance buying additional real estate after buying their first home.

In Los Angeles specifically, I've seen female investors in real estate have a huge impact on inventory and resale prices. One client of ours, Sheena, a former financial manager in cable television, said flipping one home at a time is now her full-time job. "I drop my kids off at school and go to the job site. It only takes about an hour or two of my day. I suppose it's the perfect 'mom job.'" We'll talk more about her story later in the chapter.

While house flipping may be an area of real estate investing traditionally dominated by men, women are more than ever making their presence known in this market. What are women bringing to the table that men may not be? Broadly, with exceptions of course, an attention to functionality and design-uniqueness—a hominess that a bottom-line investor may not be so apt to inject into a project, like a farmhouse sink with a geometric tile backsplash, a funky cement tile bathroom floor, or perhaps a freestanding bathtub for candlelit relaxation time or baby bathing. Buyers are very sensitive to a home's atmosphere as the place where they will raise their children or enjoy fireside chats with their partner.

Many female flippers can relate to buyers, because they are moms, too. Another client, Nicole, told me that flipping homes has been a "natural, yet exciting adventure" because the "free creativity is gosh darn thrilling! The opportunity to design with a much broader end user with whom my husband and I relate to is a dream."

The most successful renovation and rehab artists combine financial intelligence and design awareness. To be truly successful, male or female, you have to powerfully negotiate with contractors, understand permitting and plans and, last but not least, have the willingness to get your hands dirty and the capacity to fill the shoes and the dreams of the buyer with form, function, and style.

Meredith, a former television executive and now a renovation artist who works with my firm, thrives on the transformation process as well. "I like going into a place where people would walk in and say they'd 'never live in a place like that' and be able to see the vision that they don't."

Property flipping probably gets the most media coverage out of all forms of real estate investing because it can make for dramatic and envy-inducing reality TV shows. From *Master Flippers* to *Vintage Flip* there are even sub-categories of flipping shows. Flipping properties, for those of you who have cut your cable, means buying a home in need of renovation and either doing those renovations yourself or, more likely, working with a contractor and team of experts. Your aim is to turn it around and sell the property as quickly as possible for the maximum profit. To that end, there are numerous things to know and keep in mind. We are going to discuss ARV (After Repair Value) or FMV (Future Market Value), hard money loans, staging, and contractors, as well as things to consider when getting into this area of real estate investing.

KNOW YOUR MARKET

The first thing you want to do is to understand your market. As we discussed earlier, just as there is a finite and changing panorama of available partners when you go on Bumble, Tinder or Raya, the MLS will show you what it has and, trust me, there will be many options, all with tradeoffs. Your job is to find one with the least risk and most potential for return. Whether you are in Akron, Ohio, or San Diego, California, there is always a market for flipping. However, it is a good idea to start by understanding what other homes in the area are selling for, what fixers are selling for, how fast these homes are selling, and what types of homes are selling the fastest.

You can find a real estate agent through my network to help you wade through data or ask friends who have bought or sold in your area. Take some time to understand the math of flipping, which means having a solid idea of what the future market value or post-renovation value of the property will be. Don't worry—you don't have to know calculus to be able to handle this kind of math. You can find an online calculator to help you, or break out your Excel spreadsheet and run the numbers yourself based on your market research and by talking with real estate agents in the area where you are targeting your search. Calculate your target purchase price, estimated renovation costs, and other expenses, the length of time for the project, and your Future Market Value (FMV) to arrive at a realistic budget for your first flip.

Design matters. My firm, ACME Real Estate, offers a quarterly trend report for flippers to make sure they are aware of which finishes are "in" and which are "out." Make sure you have good guidance on finish or your flip will sit on the market, a generic overpriced unwanted house.

Ask your agent which neighborhoods are at the beginning of the transformation process. Look there...acquisition costs may be lower. But keep your renovation costs low, too, to accommodate the uncertainty of how desirable the property will be in a new market.

FINANCING

There are almost as many ways to finance your flip as there are items on the menu at the Thai restaurant where you meet your Bumble date. The first and most streamlined way is simply paying cash. Time and speed is key when getting into the flipping market, especially when you are in competition to buy the property. You could also draw on a home equity line of credit to generate cash for a flip. As mentioned earlier, you might also partner with a contractor who is interested in putting up the cash for a share of the sale of the property. Or maybe your aunt has always wanted to invest in real estate, but never had the courage. She might give you a cash loan, which you could pay back with interest or with an agreement for a share of the profits from the sale.

Probably the most common method used for financing flips is hard money loans. These are made either by private investors or private money lending companies which lend against the FMV of the property. They are short-term, high-interest loans that you repay immediately upon completion of the sale. Do not worry about needing great credit to get these loans, as they are not based on personal credit history. They are based on the FMV of the property you are planning to flip. These loans are not for owner occupants.

Knowing the math before you get started entails figuring out your projected budget for renovations, then what your carrying costs will be, which includes closing costs, loan repayment, permits or insurance costs, and your time frame for the whole project. Obviously, the shorter the time frame the better as this will minimize costs and maximize returns. To sum it up, financing your flip could involve one of the above methods, or a combination of all of the above. There is no one right way!

FIND A GREAT REAL ESTATE AGENT

There really is no good reason to go it alone without a real estate agent. Why? Because their guidance is invaluable. In most parts of the US, buyer representation is free of charge to the buyer and commission is only paid by cooperating commission of the listing broker. Though it's important to find a real estate agent who is investment friendly and understands your goals. That's why I've set up my nationwide referral network (**www.breakupwithyourrental. com**) so we can find a perfect match for you.

What to look for in a real estate agent? Experience, competence, commitment to the outcome, and outside the box thinking.

Warning Signs? Bad/sporadic communication, vague answers, carelessness with regard to the photography/presentation of the property to market.

Advice? Look at the agent's past listings online, read the Zillow reviews, do your due diligence. Don't just use a friend or family member.

The agent will be the connection between you and the deal.

FIND THE DEAL

I suggest getting out there and analyzing a whole bunch of potential deals before you make your first offer. Data suggests that for every twenty places seen and fifteen offers made, you might have only one or two offers accepted. Stick to your guns regarding the acquisition price.

Once you've found a place you really want to buy and your offer has been accepted, there are several possible contingency clauses you could put into your agreement. Keep in mind, the more contingencies the less likely your offer will be successful. The first is an

Appraisal Contingency, which means you can back out of your offer if the appraisal comes in at much less than you expected, or at the very least, renegotiate the contract price to the appraised value. If you are buying with cash, you will most likely NOT make the offer contingent on appraisal, as lenders order appraisals. No lender typically means no appraisal. The second is an *Inspection Contingency. This is your walkaway clause.* If the inspection of the house (highly recommended and don't try to go budget in this area) comes in with more issues than you want to deal with, you have the right to renegotiate the price, ask for credits or repairs, or cancel the deal without penalty. And finally, a *Financing Contingency,* which relates to your qualifications as a borrower. If for some reason, your financing falls through, you can cancel without penalty. Most cash deals have no appraisal, no financing contingency, and only the physical inspection contingency included.

After your offer is accepted you will wire your *Earnest Money Deposit* which, depending on what state you live in, will be held by the title/escrow company or an attorney until closing. It is applied toward your down payment. At this point, you should be drawing up your work plan for everything that needs to be done and start interviewing contractors.

Stay away from uber cheap contractors who don't guarantee their work—trust me, it is not worth the risk or the short-term savings involved. You also don't necessarily need a super high-end contractor who may only work on million-dollar homes. Only use these contractors for specialty jobs. For example, if you are flipping a $5 million house, you want to use a high-end contractor because you will get an upscale product and finish. In cheaper markets, you don't want to over-improve. You want to match the contractor to the price of the house. Most likely, your needs will be served by a middle of the road contractor who charges reasonable rates. But you will have to be very diligent about keeping tabs on their progress, or else hire a project manager, because contractors are notorious for taking much longer to do the work than they say they will.

- Avoid "time and materials" billing. Negotiate your prices based on scope of work.

- Don't let the contractor choose the finish! You need to see what finishes sell and try to make the best choices for cost that have the highest design impact.

- Do not make the final payment to the contractor until you have re-inspected their work. Once you pay them, it's hard to chase them down for unfinished or poorly finished work.

Once you have successfully completed your first renovation, hopefully on time and on budget (but don't be discouraged if all doesn't go perfectly according to plan right out of the gate), you are ready to put your house on the market and sell it. List it on the MLS through your real estate agent and stage the home. Professional staging companies are now available in most areas. Do some research! Ask your real estate agent—he/she will know who the best stagers are in your area. The staging will remain in the home for the duration of the sale, through the appraisal and physical inspection contingency removal. Staging is the "sizzle with the steak." It makes a huge difference. It creates an environment, scale, and the look of a desirable lifestyle. It creates the aspiration.

Once you've sold your flip, you could fly to Bermuda with the profits, but I recommend reinvesting that money in another flip or a rental property. Flipping houses is a higher risk investment, but like all high-risk investments, it can earn you big returns.

Meredith came to her second career in real estate after working for twenty years as a production manager in TV and film. Disillusioned and burnt out, she took what she describes as her "Eat, Pray, Love" journey to India for a couple of months to figure out what she wanted to do next. She always had an interest in real estate and had already tried her hand at two investment properties, which were long-term rentals and provided her with some passive income.

The more she thought about her next steps in real estate, the more she realized it had commonalities with her experience as a production manager. "I'm comfortable dealing with large numbers. Managing and renovating a house is just like managing the different departments of a movie." She decided to take out a chunk of her life savings and buy her first property to renovate and flip.

Meredith bought her first property to flip in January 2017 for $370,000. It was a craftsman style house that was in livable condition, but everything was in need of updating. This included plumbing, electrical, the kitchen and bathrooms, all of which came to a total of $100,000, again financed with her life savings. She sold it in May of the same year to a young family for $590,000.

Her next move was to sell her rental house, which she had bought fifteen years prior for $240,000. She was able to get $780,000, proof in the pudding, once again, that there is almost no better return on your money than real estate over time! She did a 1031 exchange, avoiding capital gains tax, in order to invest the proceeds in the purchase of a multi-family 4-plex (two 2-bedroom units and two 1-bedroom units) for $1.1 million. Her plan for this property was to renovate each unit and sell them individually. Her experience as a production manager came in handy as she created a budget using her tried and true Movie Magic Budgeting software, which she now uses for each renovation project. Even with budget projections, things don't always go according to plan. She thought she was only doing cosmetic renovations to the multiplex units, but they ended up needing completely new electrical and plumbing. She spent $150,000 renovating all four of them. She hopes to sell the 2-bedrooms for $650,000 each and the 1-bedrooms for $525,000 each.

Meanwhile, Meredith purchased two other craftsman style single-family homes, which she is planning to renovate and flip. She has learned she won't always make what she hopes on each property, so it's more important to have an idea of what her margins will be and what she hopes to sell it for at the outset of the process. "I'm very conservative with all my costs. I project my worst case scenario and work from there, but the more I do it the better I know what my margins will be."

According to Meredith, the most difficult part of the renovation process for her is the actual acquisition of each house. She focuses her efforts on a four to five mile radius of south Los Angeles where the real estate prices rise daily. "Something that would have been $350,000 six months ago is now going for $460-$475,000—and it's a completely unlivable property." House flipping is never for the faint of heart, but Meredith loves it. "My dream is to buy a church and develop it into cool condos. Now, I get up easily at 6:30 a.m. and I learn something new every day. Not one day is the same as the next."

She works with a construction manager, but handles most of the details of each project herself. However, she has gotten to the point where she needs to hire a full-time project manager in order to free up her time to look for new properties and deal with bigger picture issues that arise. Her only problem: she's too busy to find that person!

While Meredith did have experience to draw from that was a good match for real estate development and a substantial nest egg to work with, do not despair if this is not your situation and you are interested in diving deeper into real estate investment.

Sheena grew up in Ghana and now lives in L.A. She was bored in her job as a cable TV finance manager. When she bought her first house to live in, she renovated it and found she really enjoyed the process. She decided she wanted to become a property flipper, so she quit her job and apprenticed herself to a very experienced property flipper for a year and a half. She made hardly any money, but knew she would gain invaluable experience. Sheena has a husband who is supportive of her, but her property work is her own.

According to Sheena, her first pregnancy sidetracked her flipping career, but when she was ready to go back to work she turned to her father to ask him if he would help her with a loan to start investing. She knew his money was sitting in a savings account and not earning him any interest, so she offered him a more attractive prospect to make a better return on his money. He was convinced and lent her $200,000 to get started. She used this money, along with a hard money loan, to buy her first property in 2014 in South

Los Angeles for $340,000.

Sheena put $90,000 of renovations into the house, transforming it from a rundown two-bedroom into a move-in-ready three-bedroom. She worked with a draftsman to rework the internal space, creating the extra bedroom. The entire process took two months from the time she closed and she was able to sell the property for $557,000. The key to flipping, according to Sheena, is being organized and ready to hit the ground running as soon as you acquire the property. She looked at about twenty houses and put in offers on at least fifteen of them before one was accepted. Her advice: "Just remember, there is no perfect house. There will always be something wrong with it or something more you want to do to it before you sell."

Sheena has flipped six properties in the past four years as well as remodeled two houses as a favor to friends. One thing she learned is that if you happen to purchase and try to flip a historic house, be sure to leave a lot of extra time for permits to be issued. She learned the hard way that she should have researched the neighborhood more thoroughly and wasted a lot of time waiting for permits to come through. "I still paid the contractor during that time, but it ended up costing me a lot more than just waiting out the time for the permits."

When Sheena bought a duplex for $490,000 in Jefferson Park, also in South L.A., I advised her that it would be more beneficial for her to convert it into a single family home, which she did, creating a stunning four-bedroom, three-bathroom, 2,200 square foot Spanish style home. It sold for $940,000, netting her $200,000 after the $250,000 worth of renovations she put into it.

Typically, Sheena puts 20% down on her properties and uses hard money loans to finance them. These loans are common in the world of flipping as they are loans secured against the value of a property and they also have a faster closing time than a conventional loan. Time is of the essence when it comes to flipping, as your aim is to keep your carrying costs—the loan repayments, closing costs, and expenses of a renovation—down as much as possible in order to improve your return on your investment when you sell.

Sheena has also been known to use other creative financing techniques such as borrowing $75,000 from a friend who was interested in making some interest on his money and putting $40,000 worth of renovation costs on her credit card.

Sheena went to college in Montreal and lived on the East Coast for a brief stint before moving to L.A., which had always been her dream. At university, she wanted to study interior design or fashion but opted for the more practical option of management information systems. Yet, she has found herself in the creative career of renovating houses and she loves it. She has three small children and a husband who is decidedly uninterested in her real estate projects, which is fine by her.

Her biggest advice to people who want to get into flipping is to try not to sweat the small stuff and try to stick to your budget. "The only times I've exceeded my budget is when I felt the market was moving and I thought I could add more value by adding in the 36-inch range instead of the 30-inch range. It's all about being organized and racing against the market. I've made a few mistakes that maybe I shouldn't have made, but I always try my luck. I figure it always works out somehow!"

Shellown, who lives in Corona, California, forty miles south of Los Angeles and just north of San Diego, has expanded from buying her own home to live in to investing in rental properties. These properties, which are outside her markets, are cheaper to acquire. She started out by buying her first home to live in when she was only twenty-seven. She grew up in Guyana and was raised by her two aunts, whom she considers to be her parents. She moved to California at the age of thirteen to try to live with her biological mother and father, which she described as a disaster. She graduated from high school as quickly as she could and moved out at the age of seventeen.

By the time she was twenty-seven, she had been dating the same guy since she moved out of her parents' house. He wasn't interested in a future, but she always knew she wanted to buy her own place. She had been working as a healthcare consultant and saving for a while and had excellent credit. She bought a four-bedroom, two-bathroom, 1,650 square-foot, one-story home with vaulted ceilings for $367,000 in 2013. She only put 5% down because she knew she would be able to refinance in a year or two and lower her interest rate and monthly payments. She went with a higher interest rate for a lower down payment. Indeed, a year later she refinanced and got her rate down to 4.675%, she refinanced again a year later and got it down to 3.865%, and another year later got it down to 3.5%. By doing so she brought her monthly mortgage payments from $2,250 per month down to $1,967 per month. All by herself.

She started renovations immediately as everything needed a makeover. She spent $60,000 on a new kitchen, recessed lighting, crown molding, and interior painting. Shellown engaged in some creative financing to pay for it all: she had extremely high credit card limits and took out a series of 0% interest loans. While a risky endeavor, she was confident she would be able to pay it all back within the time period to avoid high interest charges. It took her a month to do the initial renovations before she moved in. Since then she has been able to afford to renovate both bathrooms, and as of 2018 the property is valued at $470,000.

In the process of renovating her first home, Shellown was bitten by the real estate investment bug. She started following popular blogs like BiggerPockets, which covers a soup to nuts compendium of every kind of real estate investing imaginable. "I have a very long commute to work in L.A. every day and I would listen to the BiggerPockets podcast on my way there and back. Once I got home I was reading real estate books, articles, and blogs to learn everything I could." Eventually, through joining various online forums she found herself in a Facebook group about stock investing, which led to discussions of real estate and the sub-category of investing in homes priced under $50,000.

Southern California is clearly not the place for this particular option, so Shellown set her sights on Middle America. Through various connections she formed online, she found her first investment property located in Cahokia, Illinois, just south of St. Louis. It was a three-bedroom, one-bathroom house, which she bought with cash for $37,500, again using her credit cards with very high limits. The house was move-in ready and she was able to quickly secure tenants, using a broker, and started getting $750 per month in rental income. Within six months, she refinanced, officially obtaining a mortgage on the property, and paid off the credit cards. At this point her mortgage payment was only $350 per month, leaving the remaining $400 as a buffer for maintenance expenses and management fees, though that only takes up a small portion of the rental payment. She secured a management company to oversee the property for 10% of the rent per month or $75/month. Shellown never went to see this property in person. She did it all online. She had no ties to Cahokia when she found it as a potential area to invest in. She trusted the recommendations of the real estate colleagues she had acquired through her various online forums.

An immense amount of due diligence has backed up all of Shellown's decisions, so she is not exactly flying by the seat of her pants. "I did my research, and for properties in this price range we're not looking for appreciation, but for cash flow. It's a C neighborhood, but my expectation is always that the rent will be equal to 2% of the purchase price." Therefore, if you buy a property for $30,000 you should aim to get $600 in rent per month.

Relationship-wise, while Shellown was not interested in waiting for another version of *The One* before she started investing in property, she actually met her current partner as a result of investing in her own financial future. She met her boyfriend in one of the online real estate groups. He lives in St. Louis and works as a real estate wholesaler. Wholesalers put a property in escrow, and then shop it to flippers, usually getting a finder's fee when they resell.

Shellown wants to continue to work in the St. Louis market as it is far more affordable than anything on either coast and has a lot of room for growth. Her aunts now live in the U.S. and her goal is to earn enough passive income from real estate to support them so they can retire. They both work in low wage, live-in positions during the week, and live with her on the weekends. The jobs are dead-ends and neither of her aunts have any retirement savings. Shellown plans to earn enough to replace half their wages within a year, then the other half after one more year. Within five years, she aims to replace her own income when her "side hustle" of real estate investing grows. She doesn't know yet if she will necessarily quit her healthcare consulting job, but she definitely wants the security that a healthy stream of passive real estate income can offer her.

To help her along that path, she recently had her best friend move into a free bedroom in her four-bedroom house. Her friend is also interested in learning the ropes of real estate investing. By giving up her expensive monthly rental and helping Shellown pay her mortgage, she is saving money towards buying her first property. The two of them hope to buy an apartment building together when they have saved enough for a down payment.

Shellown believes it's absolutely critical to have a support group of people she trusts to be able to ask questions and learn from along the way. She says transparency is extremely helpful as well. Meaning, she and her real estate investing friends share their mistakes and their triumphs and learn from each other. While not a property flipper, Shellown is proof that there is not one traditional route to successful real estate investing. Everything can be learned and you don't need to start with a huge chunk of cash. Educate yourself, find your niche that fits your particular circumstances, and the possibilities are endless.

TV and content producer Melissa is another woman who has been using real estate as a tool for economic and creative empowerment for a while now. Full disclosure: Melissa produced my TV show, *My City's Just Not That Into Me* on FYI Network, but she had a strong foothold in real estate long before that. After twenty years of living in Chicago, she was tired of the wind and cold. She built a house in Florida and will find herself mortgage free after a series of smart decisions along the way. "Real estate is the one part of my life that has always gone really well. I've had terrible luck with relationships and health issues, but real estate is the one part of my life where I've always had really good karma."

Now in her mid-forties, Melissa bought her first condo in the Lincoln Square neighborhood of Chicago when she was twenty-nine, which she claims was "absolutely the most important decision I've made in my entire life." A series of year-end bonuses helped her save for her 20% deposit on the place that she got for $185,000 in 2000. If you are in a job where you get bonuses, they are a great way to pull together a down payment because, as Melissa put it, "if you haven't already spent it in your head you can put it away and not miss it that much."

Melissa lived in her first place for ten years and sold it for $285,000 in 2010 to trade up to a condo twice its size, which she got for $506,000 in the West Loop. Her good real estate karma held and she got the place for $150,000 less than it was originally listed for, because all of the seller's previous deals had fallen through since other buyers were relying on jumbo mortgage loans, which were trickier to secure while the housing market was still recovering after the crash. This forced the seller to drop the price so she was able to buy the property while staying under the jumbo loan qualification requirement.

Melissa lived in her second condo in the West Loop for five years, during which time she went through treatment for breast cancer and started her own media production company. Then a confluence of events made her think it was time to leave Chicago. Her father was suffering from Alzheimer's disease, she felt the pull to go home to Colorado to help her mother, and then she slipped on the ice coming back from the grocery store in her neighborhood during the winter of 2014 and fractured her ankle. She remembers lying on the sidewalk in the dark, freezing night, waiting for a passerby to stop and help her. After what seemed like an eternity, someone did. She ended up needing surgery and was housebound for three months that winter because there was too much ice to risk falling during her recovery period. Around the same time, she learned her neighbor in the building had just gone under contract for his place, which was very similar to hers, for $850,000. That sealed the deal for her selling up and getting out of Chicago. She put it on the market and accepted the first offer she received, which was $800,000.

Melissa's sale and closing was fast and smooth and within two months she was living with her mother in Colorado and spending time with her father until he passed. From there, she set her sights on relocating to Florida because she wanted a warmer climate after years in Chicago. After looking at numerous places on the market in the St. Petersburg area, where she planned to move, she was unimpressed with the housing supply. This led her to research building her own place and finding a contracting company that specialized in homes that were very contemporary with great design elements and in her price range.

Fairly quickly, she went under contract with her chosen company to build her three-bedroom, two-bathroom modern ranch for $440,000, land included. She added a pool, which brought the total cost to about $500,000, which she was able to pay for in cash with the funds from the sale of her Chicago condo. Melissa is thrilled with her decision and the freedom it affords her as she begins to set up her new life in Florida. She is even moving her mother down to live with her for a while. "I've worked hard and hustled my whole life and I just don't want to have to kill myself to pay a mortgage anymore. And at the end of the day, when I look at my life accomplishments—having a beautiful home that I built, own, and live in is right up there. I'm very, very happy that I built this from scratch and by myself at the age of forty-seven."

SO MANY FISH IN THE SEA

When considering a home as an investment, whether to flip or rent out, you have to be able to answer the question: what is it that buyers want? First-time homebuyers have a short list: move-in ready, some yard, a bathtub for baby, and an open living/dining/kitchen area. But the devil is in the details—a specialty that design-savvy women understand all too well. Keep the hardwood floors and refinish them to a natural matte, avoid laminate. Use gender-neutral finishes in kitchen and bath—not too heavy on the dark colors. For example, if a backsplash is black geometric tile, make the cabinets natural wood and the countertops white. Make sure all the drawers open easily. Don't let the only bathtub be in the master. Make sure there's enough closet space in the master to accommodate modern wardrobes and shoe storage needs. A washer/dryer hookup inside the home is preferable to the garage. A rear garage that can double as a studio or overflow space adds value. These are choices you can make based on the buyers' vision of what "move-in ready" means.

In general, the most successful strategy is to research properties that have already been flipped in a particular neighborhood and see what finish they are using and then either enhance it or duplicate it. Don't make a choice that is going to create a visceral response in people when they walk in the door, like painting a wall an unusual color that is going to engender a love or hate response from people. But then you also don't want to go so neutral that it looks like corporate housing. Check out current design trends by studying the latest Ikea, West Elm or CB2 catalog, flip through Dwell Magazine.

Remember, you can make a house attractive to buyers in any market—whether it's Dayton Ohio or Los Angeles. The difference will just be in your profit margins and variances in the time to acquire, renovate, and sell. So for example, if you're working with smaller margins in Dayton, Ohio, you might choose butcher block countertops instead of quartz, because they're cheaper but they still look fresh and bright in the photos, and you might choose Ikea finishes, like a $100 light fixture as opposed to something a bit more upscale from West Elm. When your margins are smaller, you need to do more flips. Quantity is the name of the game.

To me, there is no better time for women to make their mark in the renovation world. Inventory is low, resale is high, and the spirit of home—perhaps a respite from turbulent national politics—is the perfect opportunity to use feminine insight to create the vision.

Now it's time for you to think about what in this entire real estate conversation inspires you the most. Is it buying to hold and being a landlord? Being a renovation artist? Developing a passive income aside from your regular job? Or maybe a combination of all of the above? You do not have to be a landlord or a full-time property flipper to make real estate work for you. Diversify your portfolio. Try some options on for size and see how they fit. The point is that answering these questions can help determine your course of action and get your game plan going. Maybe these construction boots were made for walking.

NOTE FROM
Courtney

Joe Mihalic of the No More Harvard Debt blog embarked on a journey a few years ago to rid himself of $91,000 worth of student loan debt in one year. He ended up doing it in seven months, through a combination of extreme frugal living, adopting a minimalist lifestyle, selling many possessions, and increasing his income in any number of ways he could.

"Don't wait to buy real estate. Buy real estate and wait."

—Will Rogers

HOW IT REALLY WORKS

I'm sure you have many questions about finances, mortgages, and the logistics of how to execute your first real estate purchase. In this chapter I'm going to share excerpts from my wide-ranging interviews with Scott Groves of the mortgage brokerage firm New American Funding and Doug Smaldino, a certified CPA and mortgage lender with Hillhurst Mortgage, both based in Southern California.

For over fifteen years Scott has been providing quality mortgage products to his clients on the Eastside of Los Angeles. After his honorable discharge from the Army in 2000, Scott attended Pasadena City College and UCLA's extension program for financial planning. Over the last fifteen years he has worked for Washington Mutual, Wells Fargo, Prospect Mortgage, Movement Mortgage, and New American Funding. Scott has received awards from multiple banks for loan production, customer satisfaction, and exemplary audit reviews. He currently serves as the branch

NOTE FROM

Courtney

Ask friends or relatives for a referral to a lender and CPA they have worked with in the past. Word of mouth and experience is always the best way to find someone you can trust. If that option is not available, interview several until you find someone who seems most attuned to your needs and long-term goals.

manager and top producing loan officer for the Los Angeles branch of New American Funding, where he and his partner are tracking to fund $150 million in personal production while also growing a branch with eight additional loan officers and six support staff. Scott is currently ranked in the top 100 loan originators for purchase mortgages nationwide.

Doug graduated from California State University Northridge with Bachelors of Science Degrees in both Accounting Theory and Practice, and Finance. He is a licensed Certified Public Accountant (CPA) in good standing with the California State Board of Accountancy. He is also a licensed real estate broker with the California Department of Real Estate. He provides financing for residential and commercial properties in California and has extensive experience in individual, corporate, partnership and international finance and tax law matters.

COURTNEY: What are some of the financing options that all soon-to-be real estate czarinas should know about?

SCOTT: I think in general there is this myth that you have to have perfect credit and 20% down to buy a house. With an FHA loan, which is a Federal Housing Administration loan, the government is basically saying homeownership is a stated goal of the country and a path for people to take towards wealth. An FHA loan requires 3.5% down and there are other lenders that offer a little bit more competitive programs with 10% down. This loan is meant for people who may have had some challenges in their credit and have been unable to get their credit score up above 650. When I do a first-time buyer seminar, the first thing I explain to people is that there are a lot of myths out there about who you have to be in order to buy a home.

There are loans out there for people who can put 1% down or for people who can put 50% down.

By the way, technically you can have at least a 500 credit score and get an FHA loan. Realistically, you need a score somewhere around that 600 mark because different lenders have different cut-offs.

DOUG: The Veterans Administration loan is one of the greatest out there if you happen to qualify, as both the rate and terms of the loan are excellent. FHA loans are also fantastic and have liberal qualifying terms. We see a lot of parents helping their kids out with gift funds for down payments, but there are stipulations with that to keep in mind. Generally, the money must come from a family member and how much you're eligible to receive as a gift depends upon the kind of mortgage you're applying for. For example, if you're taking out a conventional loan, one backed by Freddie Mac or Fannie Mae, all of your down payment can be gifted if you're putting down 20% or more. If you're putting down less than that, some of it can be gifted but some must come from your own funds, the amount depends on the individual stipulations of the particular mortgage type.

If it's an FHA or VA loan, the entire down payment amount can be gifted unless your credit score is below 620, in which case, you would have to be responsible for the 3.5% down payment yourself. Also the house you're purchasing needs to be serving as your primary residence and not an investment property.

COST AND TAX BENEFITS OF HOME OWNERSHIP

	80/10/10 Jumbo	80/10/10 Conventional	90% Single Loan - Fixed	20% Down
PURCHASE PRICE	**$500,000**	**$550,000**	**$600,000**	**$650,000**
Down payment %	20%	20%	20%	20%
Down payment amount	$100,000	$110,000	$120,000	$130,000
1st Loan Amount	$400,000	$440,000	$480,000	$520,000
Interest Rate	4.375%	4.375%	4.375%	4.375%
1st Loan Monthly Mortgage Payment	$1,997.14	$2,196.86	$2,396.57	2,596.28
Monthly Property Tax	$520.83	$572.92	$625.00	$677.08
Monthly Fire Insurance	$54.17	$59.58	$65.00	$70.42
Total Monthly Outlays	$2,572.14	$2,829.36	$3,086.57	$3,343.78
Monthly Tax Deduction (avg. Yrs 1-3)	$1,997.20	$2,174.92	$2,372.64	$2,570.36
Assumed Marginal Tax Rate, CA + Federal	38%	38%	38%	38%
Monthly Tax Savings (avg. Yrs 1 - 3)	$751.34	$826.47	$901.60	$976.74
Net Monthly Cost (After Tax Savings)	$1,820.80	$2,002.88	$2,184.97	$2,367.05

COURTNEY: Does it matter where your lender is located?

SCOTT: Although there are fundamental truths about lending, there are state-to-state differences, so it's certainly best to get in touch with a lender near where you live or plan to buy.

COURTNEY: What questions should a person ask their lender if they are self-employed, like a freelancer or actor?

SCOTT: Great question. We certainly deal with the entertainment industry a lot here in Southern California but it could also be the self-employed woman in the Midwest that owns the small bookkeeping company. Either way, the thing to talk about is your tax returns.

The question you need to ask is what is your net income versus your gross income? People in the entertainment industry seem to be the most egregious offenders of this. They say to me, "I make a hundred thousand dollars a year."

And then I say to them, "That's what was on your 1099." It's good to show that you earned that, but when you meet with your accountant and your tax professional and you put your heads together, all of a sudden that hundred thousand dollars in gross receipts and 1099 income is $40,000 in net income when it actually shows up on your IRS forms. You're going to need to re-examine the expenses you reported, like if you said 100% of your cell phone bill is used only for business and 100% of your cable bill is a business expense because you are studying your craft by watching TV and 100% of your dry-cleaning bill is for business because you only wear nice clothes to work.

I have to have this conversation all the time with borrowers where I say, "Look, I'm not judging you. I hate the IRS more than anybody. I hate taxes more than anybody, but at the end of the day when you take all those deductions what you're telling lenders is 'Hey, to produce $100,000 I need $60,000 in expenses,' and that doesn't look very good to them."

Once you write off all those expenses, the underwriter has to look at that and say, I can no longer qualify you on that $100,000 1099 income. I can only qualify you on the $40,000 net. I probably have this conversation once a day. Being self-employed does not make it intrinsically harder to get a loan. Being self-employed just generally leads to being able to be more aggressive on your write-offs, which then depresses your net income and makes it harder to qualify for a loan. A lot of this is just preplanning. If you're thinking of buying a house and you're self-employed, you probably need to be planning about a year in advance. My advice: Don't take as many write-offs two years before you plan to buy a house so that your net income on your IRS forms is larger.

If you're planning to buy a house in the next twenty-four months, I need to look at your tax returns before you file them to see how aggressively you are taking your write-offs. And yes, you might pay an extra five thousand dollars in federal taxes, but it will help you buy a house.

DO'S AND DON'TS DURING THE LOAN PROCESS

- Don't change your job before applying for a home loan. This is not the right time to become self-employed or quit your job. You want to show lenders stability, which means you'll be less likely to default on the loan.

- Don't change banks. Like your employment, you want your banking history to show stability.

- Don't buy a car or truck or any other form of transportation that you have to finance. This increases your debt-to-income ratio and that's something lenders don't want to see.

- Don't buy furniture on credit before buying your house. Like financing a car, charging big-ticket items increases your debt-to-income ratio and now is not the time.

- Don't be late on your credit card payments or charge excessively. You need a track record of responsibility to show that you can manage your money.

- Don't make large deposits into your bank accounts. Lenders like the money that will be your down payment to be sitting in your account for at least two months. What they call "seasoning," so that funds don't just appear out of the ether.

- Don't lie on your loan application. Sounds simple, right? Don't leave out any debts or liabilities or fudge your income. It's fraud.

- Don't co-sign a loan for anyone. Even if you're not the one making the payments on the loan, it increases your debt-to-income ratio.

- Don't cause inquiries into your credit. Looking for new credit translates into higher risk for lenders. If your inquiries are related to your mortgage search, it usually doesn't affect your credit score because the assumption is that you're rate shopping. But opening credit card accounts within a short period of time represents some risk and your credit score could take a hit. It's probably not a huge factor in your calculating your ability to repay a loan, but why take a chance at this juncture?

- Don't spend the money you will need for closing costs. Part of the price of financing a loan is the closing costs and you'll likely have some responsibility for paying them. Make sure you have enough for your share of the obligation.

COURTNEY: Should we be paying off our student loan debt or our car loan in order to qualify for a higher loan?

SCOTT: The perfect answer is to have no debt. Okay, that's probably not realistic but frankly set yourself up with good habits because you're about to take on this massive debt. If it's just the credit cards, get down to the ropes and get in the habit of paying them off at the end of the month. It's the very standard Suze Orman or Dave Ramsey advice—probably everybody should read one of those books at some point. You're about to take on a big expense and your payments will probably be a little bit higher than rent. You're going to have the unforeseen leak in the roof or have to replace the roof. Do anything you can to get out of the credit card trap. If you have any debt at all, the credit card should be the first to go. Get out of the habit of running up those credit card bills and living off those cards. That's number one.

Number two is student loan debt. This is actually the primary reason I have to tell clients they don't qualify for a loan. Honestly, I think it's almost criminally irresponsible that somebody who wants to become a public school teacher making $45,000 a year is even allowed to go into $200,000 in student loan debt because they went to USC or Stanford or some other private school. It really concerns me that nineteen- or twenty-year-olds are able to go into $50 to $100 to $200,000 worth of debt to get a degree from a private institution.

COURTNEY: If a person has a low interest student loan, do they have to pay it off before buying a house? Does it make a difference what size the loan is? Should they pay it down to a certain amount, if not all the way?

SCOTT: All the lenders finally caught on to this and now they say we need to know what your payment is or we need to hit you for 1% of the loan balance as your monthly payment. So if it is 1% of a quarter of a million dollars, your monthly payment on the student loan should be somewhere around $2,500 a month. And now you don't qualify because of it. But there's a lot of stuff we can do to help people fix their credit. There is a consultant approach we take to help people get qualified for a loan.

DOUG: I tell my clients to try to attack their revolving debt first, which is credit card debt, as opposed to installment debt, known more commonly as student loans. This is because revolving debt has more of an immediate impact on your credit score.

COURTNEY: How are the new tax laws going to impact first-time home buyers?

SCOTT: No effect. Especially for property flippers and people that are buying and holding property long term. There was actually a ton of net positive in the tax laws that will help those people. Buyers here in California who are already wealthy and were going to get a mortgage over $750,000 were not going to be able to write off state taxes anymore. Those people kind of got screwed out of a couple thousand dollars a year. But for 95% of home buyers there was either no change or a small net positive.

COURTNEY: What is the number one question you get from single women who are first-time home buyers?

SCOTT: The number one question is about interest rate. Shame on us as an industry that the only thing we advertise is the interest rate. This is a really big concern for single women because they know they're operating off of one income. They'll say, "Well, you know, my bank said that they can do .1% or .5% (cheaper) or I saw an online ad that said they could do 3.75%." Well, first of all, as an American you should know that anything in an advertisement is bullshit. If you see an advertisement on TV to lease a new Lexus for $299 a month, everybody seems to intrinsically understand that rate only exists because it's $6,000 upfront and I'm going to get the base model that nobody has. When I actually leave the dealership I pay $450 a month. People often don't realize there is just as much false advertising when it comes to mortgages as in every other industry.

For example, a great deal on a loan you might see on the Internet is only available with 30% down and perfect credit and you can't be self-employed. So, I let people know that the nuances of rate do not matter so much. If you try to shop at this company or that company to save an eighth of a percent on interest, it is going to come out to only $40 less a month, and it's tax deductible so it's really only $20 less a month. It's not even worth your headache. It's better to go with a company that is a trusted referral rather than to get too hung up on the interest rate.

DOUG: I agree there is way too much focus on rate. The fees are the bigger things to consider. I ask this question on a daily basis and it stumps most people: which is better, a 3.5% rate with 15% in loan fees or a 4% rate with no loan fees? It's much more important to focus on affordability, your long term goals, and tax benefits. I tell people to talk to their accountant early on in the process. Fees are ignored and people have no idea what their tax benefits might be. Even under the new tax law, if you live in a house for two out of five years of owning it, any capital gain (appreciation when you sell) you make on the house is excluded up to $250,000 if you're single and $500,000 if you're married. Also, you can write off the interest on any loan up to $750,000, which would apply to most buyers across the country. The only thing that matters is closing the loan. It doesn't matter what rate I tell you—if you can't close the loan then we've all wasted our time. That's my biggest talking point over and over again.

COURTNEY: Do you find that the majority of people are actually buying at their maximum?

SCOTT: Yes, absolutely, whether or not because they write off too much or they write off nothing and they're just a one-page W-2 employee. We try to get clients approved up to about 45% debt to income ratio.

CALCULATING DEBT-TO-INCOME RATIO CHARTS

To calculate your Debt-to-Income ratio (DTI), divide your monthly debt payment by your gross monthly income.

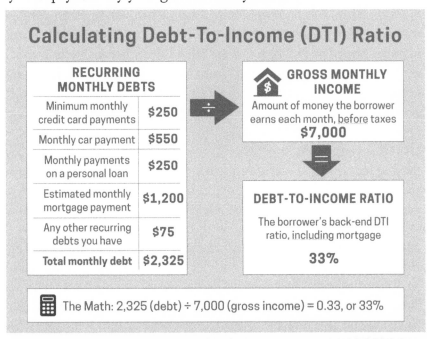

Calculating Debt-To-Income (DTI) Ratio

RECURRING MONTHLY DEBTS	
Minimum monthly credit card payments	$250
Monthly car payment	$550
Monthly payments on a personal loan	$250
Estimated monthly mortgage payment	$1,200
Any other recurring debts you have	$75
Total monthly debt	$2,325

GROSS MONTHLY INCOME
Amount of money the borrower earns each month, before taxes
$7,000

DEBT-TO-INCOME RATIO
The borrower's back-end DTI ratio, including mortgage
33%

The Math: 2,325 (debt) ÷ 7,000 (gross income) = 0.33, or 33%

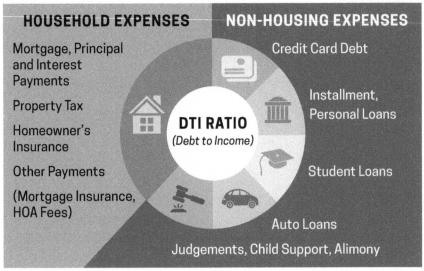

HOUSEHOLD EXPENSES

Mortgage, Principal and Interest Payments

Property Tax

Homeowner's Insurance

Other Payments

(Mortgage Insurance, HOA Fees)

NON-HOUSING EXPENSES

Credit Card Debt

Installment, Personal Loans

Student Loans

Auto Loans

Judgements, Child Support, Alimony

DTI RATIO
(Debt to Income)

I'm always amazed our company doesn't get more calls from our clients who are unrealistic and are at a 70% debt to income ratio. Inevitably, we've got to drop the interest rate or get cheaper homeowner's insurance or have them pay off a credit card to qualify.

People tend to overextend themselves and push to the absolute maximum they can afford. Then they get into a house and stop saving for the next house, so they have to sell the current house in order to have a big enough down payment to buy the next one. If you are able to save for the next house while you have your first, and you're not necessarily dependent on selling the first one, that's how people obtain real wealth going into retirement.

COURTNEY: Do you recommend single women buy real estate?

SCOTT: Yes! The biggest success story is single buyers. More often than not, they're women. I get a ton of families where the guys like taking the lead on the finances and having the first conversation, but when I have a single individual buying their first condo, it is usually a woman. That in and of itself is a success story because either women have their shit together more early in life than men do, because they're more mature, or guys are just spending all their discretionary income on cars, drinking, and dating women, or whatever. My single buyers will start with the smaller condo as the starter house. I tell them, you'll date that condo for a few years and then you'll sell it. You make a few bucks and then you'll marry the next house.

COURTNEY: Do you have a buyer's success story that you'd like to share?

SCOTT: Jessica McCool is my favorite success story because she bought her first house when she was an assistant branch manager at a bank and she was making maybe $60-$70,000 a year. She kept it for a few years and then took cash out of that house when she and her fiancé got married so she could put her husband through law school. When they sold it they had enough cash to buy a nice family home up in Newbury Park. He went on to be a very successful lawyer. They used that cash to get a reasonable mortgage on a house in the suburbs. She is a very happy stay-at-home mom with three kids, and all of it was predicated on the fact that she made a good financial decision when she was twenty-three or twenty-four. This is how real estate can work as a wealth accumulation tool. She was able to roll that initial investment into building the family life that she wanted. And you know how sad it would have been if she had waited ten years to buy the first house. They would never have gotten there. Her husband would still be working at Trader Joe's and she would still be working in a bank instead of being home with her three kids.

This is my own story: I bought a house in Cypress Park, which used to be a really rough neighborhood. It was the only place that I could afford going into 2008. I bought in August of 2008. Literally the worst possible time in the history of America to buy a house was August 2008. It was right before the crash. I paid top dollar at the time in Cypress Park, which was like $350,000. Five months later Zillow said my house was worth $180,000, so I just completely hit the ground on the biggest investment that I had ever made. But you know a home is not supposed to be an investment you care about day to day. Seven years later in 2015 I sold it for $150,000 profit.

COURTNEY: How do you deal with people's fears of "being underwater" in the market or having a house that's worth less in the future?

SCOTT: What I tell people is buy a house today and it may be worth zero tomorrow, but you can still rent a room and make passive income from that house. However, you invest $100,000 in a stock portfolio and it goes to zero it's worth exactly zero. The point is nothing is without risk. But historical data supports the fact that people who hold onto their homes through changing market cycles, make much more of a profit in the long run. Being "underwater" is simply a function of timing the sale of your home. Yet people, as of this writing, are willingly throwing money at Bitcoin and cryptocurrencies. However promising these investments might look now, one thing is for certain: you can't pitch a tent on them.

So my friend was busting my chops over a quarter of a percent on interest rate and I said, "You know what? I know you have Bitcoin investments and you're sinking $200,000 in that because it's gone up and down 2,000% in the last six months. And you know, and I know, that it's a speculative investment and it could go to zero tomorrow and they aren't worth anything, so buy something real—buy a house. And if your house goes to zero you can still live in it. If you're invested in a property that goes to zero you'll still have a roof over your head. That's not a bad thing. And then it always comes back. I have these conversations whenever I hear somebody complaining about the cost of rent, especially in metropolitan areas.

COURTNEY: What about people who still think renting is a better deal than owning because of the risk?

SCOTT: Chicago, L.A., Nashville, Austin—rent has never gone down in a major metropolitan area, even during the major real estate crash in 2009. Guess what? Rental costs went up because there were more renters than there were buyers. So when I hear somebody complain about the cost of rent, I say, "Yes, rent goes up, but that person bought a house five years ago and got a thirty-year fixed rate mortgage. Their payments are never going to go up ever. And your rental payment is going to go up 100% of the time."

DOUG: Yes, in California at least, rents are so insane it is actually cheaper to own than to rent.

SCOTT: Your first 10 years of owning you're paying mostly interest so if you're going to rent your property out, after 10 years is a great time to do it because your principal is getting paid down rapidly after year 10. These days, people can really take advantage of the sharing economy, like with Airbnb they can rent out a room in their house if they need extra help paying the mortgage.

97

To circle back to my earlier point about saving for the next house, those people who are able to do that will be forty-five years old, looking back and saying, "I bought my first house in my twenties, it is now paid off and it's spinning off $3,000 a month in rent. Then I bought my next house when I got engaged. That's almost paid off and it's paying me $4,000 in rent and we've only got ten years left on the mortgage on our forever house. Then we'll own $1.5 million in real estate and then we'll be $5,000 a month cash flow positive. With that and Social Security, we can pretty much retire." That's the long game people can play. But people lose track, myself included, and then kick themselves in the ass when they're looking at forty and they're not in a good place financially.

COURTNEY: Where is the best place to put your extra money if you're a renter who wants to become a homeowner or investor and have never done it before?

SCOTT: Cash or cash savings. Everything else is too speculative for the short term if you want to buy a house within the next one to five years.

COURTNEY: Could you explain the difference in the details on these loans—the 85/15/5 and the 80/10/10 funding options/loans?

SCOTT: A lot of these mortgage options are going to change because of the new tax law. A lot of borrowers used to use second mortgages—lines of credit—which is the 15/5 or 10/10 part of that question. Basically anything to bridge the gap so that the first loan would be 80% of the loan value. They would put some money down and then they would take out a line of credit to basically supplement their down payment.

DOUG: Again, this is why I suggest people talk to a CPA even before they reach out to a lender or broker. There is a lot of education that needs to take place on all the options. Find a CPA who is savvy about real estate, which should not be hard to find. It's like you have to eat your meatloaf before you can have your chocolate cake. But most of the time, people want the chocolate cake first—the property they fall in love with—then it's rush, rush, rush trying to line up a lender, so important tax considerations are missed. Do it the other way around and you won't regret it.

COURTNEY: Are there any loan products for people who are not owner-occupants but investors where you could put down less than 30%?

SCOTT: There's a lot of wiggle room if you're buying investment single-family residences—most of the time you can just put 15% down—but if you're looking at an investment model of larger units to rent out, you're going to have to put between 25% and 30% down because it's a higher risk to the lenders.

DOUG: We love to see first-time buyers considering a duplex, which is a great option. You live in one side and rent out the other, using that rental income to pay your own mortgage down. This can set you up very well if you want to build a real estate investment portfolio. When you're ready to move to a bigger place, you might not need to sell at all but simply rent out both units and use whatever appreciation you've gained on the property to fund your next purchase. Also, anything in the two- to four-unit property range qualifies for a residential mortgage. Above that it gets into commercial mortgages. So you could get an FHA loan, with 3.5% down, to purchase a duplex or similar up to $850,000. That's a pretty amazing option.

COURTNEY: What's your parting advice for our readers?

SCOTT: Call your lender a year in advance. Seriously, your search for your home should actually start with your lender.

DOUG: Consider the tax implications of ownership before anything else and be working on your credit score. Know what a credit score is and what affects it. More often than not I see people with bad scores just because they've been careless with their finances.

COURTNEY: Great advice. And people need to realize those online mortgage calculators aren't necessarily correct.

SCOTT: Right. The online mortgage calculators will say you're approved for $802,000 but in reality that's not true. You need to talk to a real live lender.

The last thing I want to talk about here is the technology shift. Leading up to 2009 it was very, very easy to qualify for a loan. If you had a pulse and a legal social security number you could get a loan. Because the mortgage industry hadn't quite caught up with technology yet it was still very hard to *apply* for a loan, because you had to come into the office in person and bring in a copy of your ID, and if you were using tax returns you had to photocopy all your tax returns. I would hold onto your original tax returns so you couldn't go down the street and also apply at Bank of America. They made it difficult to apply for a loan. Now that dynamic has completely switched. We've got Quicken online and we've got the start-up mortgage companies that are really tech companies masquerading as mortgage companies. So now it's super easy to apply for a loan. We had someone yesterday who called us and said, "I applied at eBay and Loan Depot, Lending Tree, and Quicken. And now I want to play with who gives me the best rate."

What that person doesn't realize is that while it is easy to apply for a loan right now, it is very, very hard to qualify for a loan, a big difference. What matters is that you get approved, and a skilled and knowledgeable lender will know how to structure the loan and tell your story to the bank so that you have the best chance of being qualified. So rather than shopping around for the best rate, shop around for a lender who is trustworthy, understands your situation, and is a good match for you.

MORTGAGE LENDING TERMS

Conforming: A mortgage loan that conforms to Freddie Mac and Fannie Mae guidelines.

Jumbo Loan: A mortgage loan above conventional, conforming loan limits, as determined by Freddie Mac and Fannie Mae (above).

ARM: Acronym for an Adjustable Rate Mortgage where the interest rate of the outstanding balance fluctuates throughout the life of the loan or for a fixed period as agreed upon at the outset of the loan.

Cap: This controls how much your interest rate on an ARM can change. There are three different kinds of caps--Initial, Subsequent, and Lifetime. Initial determines how much the rate can increase the first time it adjusts, the Subsequent cap determines how much it can increase in adjustment periods that follow, and the Lifetime cap determines how much the rate can increase in total.

Equity: The difference between your home's market value and your unpaid loan balance.

Hard Money: A type of asset-based loan financing through which a borrower receives funds secured against real property. This kind of loan is most often secured through private financing. Investor-friendly high interest short-term loan.

Portfolio Lending: A portfolio lender originates mortgage loans and also holds a portfolio of their loans instead of selling them on the secondary market.

Now that you have a better idea of what some financing options might look like and you are armed with more information on where to begin, I am hoping that the prospect of buying your first home is seeming ever more doable. Truly, I think we take on more risk when we get married than when we buy a home by ourselves. If the house doesn't work out for you or you feel that you got in over your head, you can sell it or rent it out. It's a transaction involving a piece of property and moving money from one bank to another. It does not involve the messy emotions and heartbreak of divorce.

Meet with a lender as soon as you possibly can. Meeting with a lender will give you a clear financial picture and help you start planning to buy a house within the next year or two.

"The best investment on Earth is earth."

–Louis Glickman

CHAPTER 7

HOW TO KNOW WHEN IT'S TIME TO BREAK UP

This we know: life is impermanent. Phases and cycles come and go—in our lives, in the stock market, in the housing market. A trip through newspaper headlines dating from the 1800s to today illustrates just how many times the media has called "doomsday" on the real estate market. And what have we learned? What makes the difference in your ultimate bottom line is when you sell, not when you buy. The people who held on during the bust years of the 1970s and did nothing were the ones who made the most in the long run when they sold thirty years later. For our purposes, we're concerned more with the five- to seven-year time span. Play to win by seeing the big picture and being flexible within the parameters of changing market conditions. Our more recent real estate recovery has *not* been a bubble in the way the last one was. People who are buying now are predominantly not buying with low money down loans. And if you are selling in better conditions than when you bought, you will prosper. Thirty-year loans are front-loaded with interest, that is, your monthly payment will be mostly interest for the first ten years. If you are able to hold onto your home but you want to move, turn the property into a rental starting at year ten, at which point a higher portion of your monthly mortgage payment pays down your principal. The combination of your principal reduction, the tenant contributions, the low interest rate when you purchased, and the appreciating market should result in greater profit when the right time to sell DOES arrive.

What is your REAL reason for selling? If you're not going to make any profit at all, consider holding onto it. But if you're going to make substantial profit it could be good to sell—*if* you use that money to buy something even better. Headlines can be both alluring and fear inducing. The media knows all too well that the fluctuations of the real estate market hit home (no pun intended) and make sensational headlines, providing plenty of click bait and newspapers sold. Sometimes it does seem too good to be true— buy a house for $400,000 in 2016 and in 2018 it's worth $600,000. Keep in mind, the law has recently changed with regard to capital gains tax, this is the tax you pay on profits from the sale of a residence (primary, secondary, or investment). The taxes are calculated as the total sale price minus the original cost of the property, depreciation and improvements. The main stipulation is that you have to have lived in the property two out of the five years before you sell it. Even better? You can rinse and repeat with another property. It is not a once in a lifetime option as it was before 1997. The new capital gains tax law dictates that when selling your primary home, you can exclude capital gains up to $250,000 in profit for single-filers and $500,000 for married filers. A *capital loss* is when you sell the property for less than you bought it for, which you can often deduct from your taxes owed.

IT'S NOT JUST LOCATION, BUT LOCAL

While the old adage about real estate is "location, location, location," and this remains true, what is often overlooked is that real estate is also extremely local. Meaning, the market within a half-mile of the property's address is the most important guidance available. As mentioned earlier, the media is fond of scaring people to death. Check national headlines about the real estate market against those in your area.

Such media hype, as you can see from the old newspaper headlines in this chapter, can cause people to short sell their property when they could have held onto it and eventually made a formidable profit. The media, however, seem to only interview economists and construction companies when trying to take the pulse of the market—not real estate agents. For example, in Los Angeles and Washington, D.C., there isn't a lot of new construction, so obviously a new home builder's opinion wouldn't be the best measure of the health of the market. Economists also get it wrong. Watch the movie *The Big Short*. It is the story of how a small group of contrarian investors bet against the crash of sub-prime mortgages that no one else saw coming in 2008. The reality is that the people who did nothing (by not selling) during the global financial crisis are the ones who ended up making the most profit when the market recovered.

You need to be informed of the real risk you are taking in holding or selling. You should only sell if the profit you stand to make is going to turn your money another way that is going to make you more money. Otherwise, hold onto your principal residence and rent it out and the lender will count that income toward the qualifying income for your next purchase. You could take out a home equity line of credit to make improvements, or do a cash-out refinance. Most lenders will limit how much equity you can cash out, usually no more than 80% of the value of your home. If your home is worth $300,000, your maximum refinance would be $240,000, so if you've paid down your mortgage to $250,000 you would be limited to cashing out $10,000.

Remember this: a buyer usually feels like she's overpaying, and sellers always feel like they are leaving money on the table. That's a given no matter the price or the market. The right time to buy or sell is going to be largely determined by your own circumstances and your local real estate market. Just don't count your imaginary chickens until they're hatched. For example, if you list your home in Ohio for $250,000 and you're attached to that price but end up selling it for less than that, you will feel like you lost money. But if you have a good team in place and a long-term strategy, the longer you hold, the more likely you will be to make the profit you desire.

105

Heidi is a great example of someone who started over from zero and is now not only a homeowner but getting into real estate investment by purchasing her first rental property. Heidi was married with two small children, and living in Los Angeles, when everything began to head south for both her marriage and finances. After her divorce, she was forced to borrow money from her best friend and buy a one-way ticket for her and her children back to her native Wisconsin. It was not a situation she ever thought she would find herself in. "There I was, living at my mom's at that wonderful ripe age of thirty-six."

After years living the actor's life and then starting a business with her husband, Heidi had to reinvent herself from the bottom up. She started with a restaurant job and a rented apartment for $450 a month. She and her ex-husband had to foreclose on their assets in California and most everything was in her name as the primary credit holder. Her credit score at that point was a dismal 450. But she had a goal because she knew she wanted to own her own home again. She began working with a credit repair agency to slowly rebuild her credit.

Eventually, she also got a much better paying job, first as an insurance broker, then by getting into pharmaceutical sales. She credits her best friend with supporting her and giving her that extra push when she needed it. After some time, her score was repaired enough so that she was able to lease a car. While Heidi was going to opt for a modest choice, her friend insisted she go for the Mercedes. "She told me I needed a reliable car and it was worth it—it had a bumper to bumper warranty on everything." As soon as she had the car, which she had to pinch herself to believe she could actually afford, her friend said, "Now it's time to get you a house!"

After a short stint of house hunting, Heidi did indeed find a house she could afford for $186,000. It was move-in ready with three bedrooms and one bath. She put a down payment of $7,000 on the house and three years later it is valued at $215,000. Meanwhile, her salary has increased which enabled her to save towards a deposit on a rental property so she could put down 30% and not withdraw any equity from her own home. She found a duplex and she plans to rent out both units. Heidi views it as her retirement nest egg. Now forty-seven, she says, "I don't have any of the things that my colleagues or other people my age have been working towards for years and years, like a 401k. The only thing I find solid right now is property."

In Heidi's case, her marriage ending was liberating even though the road to reclaiming her financial future was not easy. "I really think that my whole life I was under the illusion that I was worth nothing and couldn't get anything on my own. Finally, having the children was the first wake-up call and then my mom said to me, 'Just grow up and take care of these two alone. They'll get used to it. It's not going to happen with him.' God forbid if I would have stayed. I think I would have sunk."

Heidi's ex-husband came out to visit her kids a couple of years ago and upon seeing her house asked her, "Who helped you buy it?"

Heidi relished her response, which was, "No one."

Kate, also in her forties, is a single, practicing psychiatrist in Chicago who recently purchased her third home on her own. Her experiences with buying real estate have not always been smooth sailing, but she would contend, always better than renting. When she came back to Chicago after college to start medical school, her parents helped her buy her first place. When she relocated to New Hampshire for her residency she bought her second house, even though it took a year to sell her house in Chicago. In the middle of her stint there she decided to switch specialties and moved to North Carolina. It was just before the financial crisis of 2008 and it took her three years to sell her house in New England. She rented from a friend in North Carolina while she saved for her next purchase.

Without any warning, her friend sold the house out from under her, which hadn't even been on the market, and she had six weeks to move. She decided it was time to return to Chicago as her father had passed on and her mother was not in good health. She was paying nearly $5,000 a month towards her mother's care costs, which was making it hard for her to save for a down payment. Finally, she was able to get her mother's care covered by insurance, which freed up some of her income.

Once she received her pre-approval letter from her lender (up to $450,000) she started looking at houses on Redfin and she found something that she felt was just right for her very quickly. She made an offer on a single family home in the western suburbs of Chicago for $379,000 and ended up paying $375,000, which included $5,000 in seller credit (the seller contributed $5,000 toward the costs of closing the loan at settlement). She put down 3.5% with an FHA loan. She had been hoping to get a Physician's Loan (a type of loan available to doctors with a very low interest rate and fees) but she needed a credit score of at least 720 and hers was only 706, because she had fallen behind on some remaining student loan debts while paying for her mother's care.

According to Kate, her latest purchase, more than the other two, made her feel very empowered. "I did this completely by myself. I came up with the down payment, found the people to help me, and I didn't have my parents giving me seed money or guiding me. What I was particularly happy with is when I felt like somebody wasn't working with me, I didn't work with them anymore. I said that's it, we're done."

Kate also fought against what she calls the natural tendencies of her Greek heritage, which resulted in her dismantling the many ingrained messages from her childhood about buying property only when you get married. She lost count of the number of times her elders would ask, in so many words, "When are you going to stop being a doctor and settle down and have a family?" She still struggles with superstitions around whether forging ahead and buying her own place is not allowing for the possibility of a partner in her life. But I believe the evidence in this book tells a different story. Kate has nothing to worry about.

WHAT TO DO WITH IT ONCE YOU'VE GOT IT

Suppose you've made some money in real estate and maybe you own one, two, or more properties. Just as you needed a great broker and mortgage lender to help you conduct your real estate transactions, you want to make sure you also have a great financial team on board. This would include, depending upon the complexity of your situation, a bookkeeper, accountant, attorney, and also a trusts and estate attorney.

Most people, especially when they are young, do not stop and think about what would happen to their assets, or their Facebook account, should they die prematurely. Whether or not you have children, but even more so if you do, it's imperative that you make plans about what will happen to your money when you are gone. Zach Dresben, a trusts and estates attorney at Kramer Law Practice in Los Angeles, says, "A good piece of advice for women, and women in families or with children in particular, is that they seek legal counsel in the context of asset protection. Who will make financial or healthcare decisions if they unexpectedly cannot make them themselves?" If you were to pass on unexpectedly, where would your assets go? Who will take care of your kids?

Sure, we're all invincible super women who plan to be sipping mojitos poolside when we're eighty and don't want to slow down on the way there to think about these things. But the price of not doing so is too high. Your assets could end up stuck in probate court and cost your loved ones thousands in needless bureaucratic fees, not to mention what could happen if clear guardianship wishes were not laid down with regard to your children.

Zach also stresses the importance of getting your financial team familiar with each other and able to collaborate successfully. In fact, he says you should encourage them to speak to one another as it helps them to have a better understanding of all aspects of either your business or your financial interests. They may also be able to give you referrals for other professionals who you might want to add to your team at some point. If this all sounds overwhelming, it doesn't need to be. Just start with a good accountant, whom you will definitely need, and a good attorney, who you will probably need at some point in your life.

Though none of us like to think of the unthinkable, in our digital age, it is especially important to take the time to do so. It's a prudent idea to at least have all your passwords to all your accounts in a safe place, or with a trusted loved one, should the unlikely ever come to pass. There are even services available now that will do this for you: mylifeandwishes.com was created by Jon Braddock, author of *Click Here When I Die!* It is an online service and portal where you can securely upload your will and all your online profiles and passwords which can be shared with your loved ones if you were to pass on unexpectedly.

No one *wants* to think about these things, but when you start to own assets of any kind, and especially if you have kids, it's time to put on the big girl pants and do the right thing, which means protecting our assets and our loved ones with estate planning, no matter if you're worth $100,000 or $1 million.

YOUR FIVE- TO SEVEN-YEAR PLAN

Rid yourself of the old-world mindset about real estate that permeates much conventional "wisdom." Counter the advice of the media and cultural zeitgeist. Namely, don't wait for *The One* before you buy your first home. Arm yourself with the knowledge that you can take action without regret—that there will be no perfect house and that no decision is irrevocable. The perfect house is the one you can afford when you are looking to buy that ticks most of your boxes. We are looking for "Mr. Right Now."

Also, holding onto your property for longer than two to three years, instead of just trying to pull out $50,000 by selling sooner, is your best chance of seeing a much greater profit. Remember, it doesn't always make financial sense to sell just because you're ready to move to another area or upgrade to more space.

People are often over-focused on paying off their mortgages as soon as possible, even though doing this takes money out of your pocket, rather than letting the market appreciate and allowing your asset to grow in value. When you are just getting started in real estate, whether it's only for your own home or an investment property, your goal is to turn your $1 into $2 of buying power. Your real money is more valuable in your pocket today than in the future, due to inflation. Use your money to make money.

PROS OF PAYING DOWN DEBT	CONS OF PAYING DOWN DEBT
Lower the amount of interest you pay on the mortgage. Over the duration of the loan you will save a lot of money by making extra principal payments. A simple example would be if you had a $100,000 mortgage and a 4.5% interest rate. If you paid an additional $100 per month you would save a whopping $26,377.36 over the life of the loan.	**Liquidity is Lessened** There is comfort in cash in the event of an emergency. If you put all your cash into repaying mortgages, you could be putting yourself in a difficult spot if something unexpected comes up.
Quicker Route to Equity Paying off the loan quicker allows you to amass equity in the property faster.	**Fewer Tax Benefits** You can write off the interest expense on your taxes but the IRS won't let you write off your principal payments.
Increased Flexibility A paid off mortgage brings options like a HELOC, or Home Equity Line of Credit, which you would not be able to acquire on an investment property. This can be a great tool if you need fast cash or to increase your investment possibilities.	**Growth is Slowed** By paying off your mortgage(s) faster, you are removing the possibility of investing in another rental property.

To review, the first thing you're going to do, if you haven't already, is to assess your current situation—your mental and emotional state. Have you run through your "what-if" scenarios and addressed any lingering fears or doubts? Once these are taken care of, address your financial situation. Are you in a position to buy now? Or what do you need to save for a down payment? And do you want to buy a place to live in or keep renting and buy an investment property? Try your hand at flipping? Finally, consider multiple locations, talk to the professionals in that specific area, study the local market to find out what is being sold and what your options are. Don't limit yourself to buying only where you live.

A house can be a creative endeavor, as much as a novel or a painting. It is something you can put your individual touch on by choosing your style, the fit and finish, landscaping, the vibe. I believe women have a special relationship with invention and creativity, but in the past this was not always a financially lucrative interest. Now the creative possibility and profit of creating a home is available to anyone at any price point, whether you're single or married, childless or you have a brood. If you want to be part of this revolution, the door is open to you. Visit **www.breakupwithyourrental.com** and I'll put you in touch with someone from my network in your area.

Breaking up with your rental is ultimately about learning how to trust yourself—how to trust your gut—and take responsibility for your financial future. Your power and potential for growth is not only within reach, it is in your hands now. You don't need anyone to do it for you or even with you. It's fine to embark on this journey with a partner, but it is not a requirement. Release yourself from thinking that it is. The one thing that successful people have in common is high risk tolerance, risk big to win big. Cliché as it is, *without risk there is no reward.* And for you, that risk might just be entitling yourself to consider giving up your rental to build your real estate empire. Take it from me, I was there. And there is no better lover than a hot home on Redfin.

HAPPY HOUSE
HUNTING!

Courtney

ON THE JOB

Tony Styler

He's locked into position of trust

By Brian Tucker
Of The Journal

People think Tony Styler because he thinks like a crook.

"When it comes to security, we have to think like crooks," says Mr. Styler, an employee of Lang Locksmith Ltd., 6903 82nd Ave.

We have to be as smart or smarter than a burglar. The only way to do that is to think like one.

If people think a locksmith only fixes and replaces locks, they're wrong. He's actually a security consultant.

In fact, a locksmith may do anything from breaking doors to installing security alarm systems to servicing entire glass-enclosed locked safes. It all depends on his experience.

As a relative newcomer to the locksmith business with two years of experience, Mr. Styler has tackled most of a locksmith's chores, except for safe work. He's opened two safes, but he says he was lucky.

Some locksmiths 'have a feel' for safes and are as adept as safecrackers. But, it takes a lot of practice and for the moment, his activities are confined to changing combination numbers which involves servicing and cleaning the locking mechanism.

Every job is different, and the variety's one of the things Mr. Styler likes about being a locksmith. Another is the kind of people that trust.

Homeowners leave their keys with him, thus entrusting him with their valuables. And businessmen tell him things they wouldn't dare reveal to others.

For example, he might be told that a top-selling executive was either leaving or was being fired. If that was the case, Mr. Styler would suggest that the business have its safe combinations changed.

To protect that trust, locksmith firms run checks on prospective employees for police records and on each determination.

He admits he could use his talents for criminal activities but says few locksmiths ever turn to crime. Part of the reason why is that locksmiths appreciate the way people trust them.

Being a locksmith can be a blessed bag of laughs and tragedy, Mr. Styler says. A locksmith who freed a honeymoon couple from a locked bathroom.

Sad side of job

On the other hand, they also pick locks for prying looking for suicide and murder victims, or change locks for rape victims.

Mr. Styler, 30, learned and the father of two, lives in Millet, about 32 miles south of the city, and got into the locksmith business by accident. He happened to be working as a maintenance supervisor of a hotel being serviced by Bob Lang, a master locksmith.

It takes about eight to 10 years for someone to be locksmith's full bag of tricks, he says. A locksmith works on the job where there are no customers — a locksmith is available, according to Mr. Styler.

Mr. Styler cares about Ed Lang a year for his job that usually takes him out of the office. He works from a panel truck, equipped in the back with a tire key cutter, tools and panel goggles, among other things, and a two-way radio, linking him with the office.

A typical day might start with a call from a distressed customer who's locked the keys in a house trailer. Within a minute, he has picked the lock with two sharp instruments. For that, he charges $15, which includes driving time.

When a customer may leave the keys in the car and Mr. Styler has to drive to a stopping centre to help out. Even Mr. Styler has forgotten his keys, but unlike most of us, he was able to pick the lock with a pin.

Next, he's summoned by a trust who wants his apartment door lock changed after a rash of burglaries nearby. As the number of break-and-enters spiral, city locksmiths appear to have more business than they can handle.

Some locks 'garbage'

Most of the houses here, the locks are garbage, he says, gesturing toward a row of houses as he's driving by.

To some of the new houses, I blame contractors. They'll build an $150,000 house and install a $6 lock. A good dead-bolt lock, which has a metal bar about an inch thick, costs $10, while a good knob-set lock costs about $10.

A dead-bolt lock with a metal bar less than as half-an-inch thick is very poor for a burglar with a set of eye-grips.

Other firms in a home's defence against burglars include weak doors, poorly-secured windows and door frames. Some people think door chains make them secure, but it's one of the falsest senses of security there is.

Land woes stall housing hopefuls

By Jim Sentania
of the Journal

Co-operative housing projects could provide serious headaches by next year for hundreds of Edmonton families if any governments would make land available for co-op projects says Lynn Hantley of Communitas.

Communitas, a publicly and privately-funded agency in Edmonton, is now working with 11 groups interested in co-op projects.

Miss Hantley says most of these groups have been turned down since June, and many more groups would develop if land were available.

But land prices in the city have skyrocketed out of the price limits set on co-op financing, and for the provincial government to keep land to those.

B.C. has a program whereby the province will buy land and lease it to co-ops and it would be logical for Alberta to consider this program, she said.

Edmonton Public Affairs Commissioner Alf Savage said in August the city is developing a policy of leasing city-owned land in Mill Woods to co-op groups.

Continuing co-op development, some local groups have formed building co-ops. This involves several families dedicating their labor free to help each other member build his own house, thereby eventually coming to the individuals involved.

Miss Hantley estimates

ge Block Bros. Real Estate Services Ltd., estimates the land to accommodate an average town house unit would cost about $6,700 at today's prices.

Construction land is going for about $120,000 an acre in the city and $80,000 an acre in outlying areas, like Leduc, he said. At an average density of about 10 units per acre the town house lots would sell for about $4,500.

Miss Hantley says the co-op land system is the answer for the provincial government to keep land to those.

and accordingly

But land prices in the city have skyrocketed out of the price limits set on co-op financing, and for the provincial government to keep land to those.

as most as 150 co-op units would be built by as many as now, and it's land becoming available.

Once more co-ops are built, the area may show more for a kind of decentralized labor, with more and more people becoming members of co-ops.

I'm sure we could have a new group forming every week or two if the land was there, she said.

Mr. Nielsen says individual land operations are real estate companies are responsible for escalating land costs. The company would look favorably upon any plan to lower land and township prices, because many home buyers are now being priced out of the market.

ago, says there are people of his group who also believe co-ops must start building new homes and construction costs now even more. They suggest members do more labor themselves to keep costs below $40,000 a unit.

We have one member who is in the construction business and has helped build several town home type developments, he said. He's only getting pressure on the group to put up some and go out and buy land now, even if labor costs rise.

But Mr. Sharman has asked the six families in the group to show more participation. He says they should think in terms of building no sooner than two years from now and to behave

Keegano, above, is the city's only existing co-op housing development, but several groups are interested in co-op projects, though they are stalled by the availability and price of land.

It's mind over matter in fat-fighting game

By Bob Cohen
Southam News Services

TORONTO — There's a new fat-fighting game in town.

It doesn't have a name, but want to play to win, you must pin your skills in my, too no corporate manner.

Said then, you much apply with ascetic determination. In the person you're interested in selling and planning but is way.

The game has been Weight Watchers International psychologist Richard B. who has just finished a two-year at the University of British Columbia or diet-graphics loss in his speciality.

Yes, you are what you eat, says Dr. Stuart, but what you eat especially how much — bound up with your behavior.

So while you hang on the way, saving are on your food, you'd better keep the other on your habits.

Dr. Stuart has written a dozen pamphlets for Weight Watchers suggesting ways to change weight-gaining eating behavior. They concern nothing unusual, he said. In a recent interview, but they all pull together a lot of thinking that has thickened out in the last decade.

In the fast indulgence he writes, watch out for the food you bring home. Make a shopping list, stick to it, and shop "only after you have had a good meal and are in a relatively relaxed frame of mind.

Once the food is through the door, it is critically important to know when you are genuinely hungry and to position yourself near eating.

If you want more properly in the periods the heart, Dr. Stuart suggests: always use plan that worked for you, one such conclusions

So when you get more point, however, don't eat for 15 minutes. If you feel you must after that, make sure you hold "is not one of your favorites.

How to calm down? Wrap your utensils at a napkin and after you sit down, wait three minutes to start. If there has been pre-meal chit chat at

the kitchen is out of sight, and confined.

When it comes down to preparing food, "make a rule not to eat anything until you are ahead of your plate."

Then fasting is unnecessary. Did anybody's children even the longer the plate had too little salt.

Cut from a seven-inch salad plate instead of a nine-inch dinner plate. It will seem full with less on it. Switch from nothing by leaving the service dishes out of reach. And let every piece take his or her own servings.

For an absolute finale, he insists: about stretching the meal out. Most overweight people he maintains, eat far too to be helped.

No matter how much food we eat, it takes approximately 20 minutes for our stomachs to signal our brains that we have had our fill. The longer it takes you to eat your normal portion, the more likely you are to be satisfied.

salts and stick to the basics — carefully-prepared meats and fish. Don't look at the menu. Ask for what you want. Come first to avoid the "one too complete."

Call ahead

If you're going to a friend's home for dinner, "call ahead to ask about the menu. Ask for your hostess's help in making small changes, or you can enjoy a light meal.

If there is no fruit for dessert, hold your coffee cup in one hand or find another way to keep both hands busy.

If you feel yourself about to eat for a helping of problem dessert, excuse yourself for a moment, go to the rest room, and try to brush your teeth or away from the table.

Who it all adds up to, then, is simply mind over matter watching poor habits that we have had and not the time it takes to eat your food.

But, as Dr. Stuart hints, there are some tricks to prime the mind

newly-announced. Nobody programs, he said.

As a result the only solution for commercial developments is to develop quickly their minds on.

Don Sherman, a Wormald Alberta College instructor who is a spokesman for Seregate, a continuing co-op group turned its minds

aerial advantages. The group hopes to maintain average monthly payments at less than $200, he said.

But there are other advantages.

Co-op members coordinate the work of architects and contractors and so have a direct hand in designing their future home.

Judge Francoise Laporte

After tragedy, a new role

MONTREAL (CP) — Francoise Laporte often speaks of her happiness in the role of wife and mother during her 24-year marriage to Pierre Laporte, the Quebec minister of labor and immigration assassinated in October 1970.

Mrs. Laporte also speaks with pride of her new role as a judge of the Citizenship Court of Canada. She feels, as well, that Pierre Laporte would be proud of the progress of their three daughters, Claire, 24, and son Jean, who is 19%, and a man.

New Canadian regularly appear before Judge Laporte to take the oath of citizenship in a downtown Montreal courtroom. She feels she meets their works in advance to her adjoining office to extend friendly greetings.

"Pierre often said we should give immigrants more than a doughnut and a cup of coffee after their arrival at Dorval airport," Judge Laporte told a reporter after her appointment to the court in March 1972.

Though Judge Laporte, 51, declared to be interviewed at present on the fifth anniversary of the terrorist kidnap crisis that took the life of her husband, she has described earlier how training about was followed by a desire to be of service.

"I was very close to my children and they were through the period with me, that molded us into one again. I have received so much in the past that I felt the time was right for me to give something to society

There is no bitterness in pitying her teacher. Her parental home.

In the courtroom, I wear the costume of office that my husband — the robes he never wore. And it's my way.

By the time Mr. Laporte took a few degree in 1946, he had already started work as a journalist with the Montreal newspaper Le Devoir and later went into politics without ever practicing law.

Francoise Laporte received the old robes from a closet and immersed herself in immigration laws and problems when she was offered the new title one of her children and helped her through period and court here. The Quebec international society had cried ended up the past that I felt the time was right for me to give something to society December 1970

prying art teacher that married Edward Axel, a young lawyer and now a taking a course at England's Oxford University.

Jean, a student at College Notre-Dame, already has ideas about what a career. He wants to be a politician.

Francoise Laporte has made public appearances honoring her husband's memory, including opening of the Pierre Laporte Bridge at Quebec City, the Pierre Laporte School in Toronto and a park named for him in St. Hubert where he was slain.

She married deeply in the 1971 when Pierre Laporte's name was detained in respects of political-order world-connections.

Pierre always knew how to defend himself, she said in a statement.

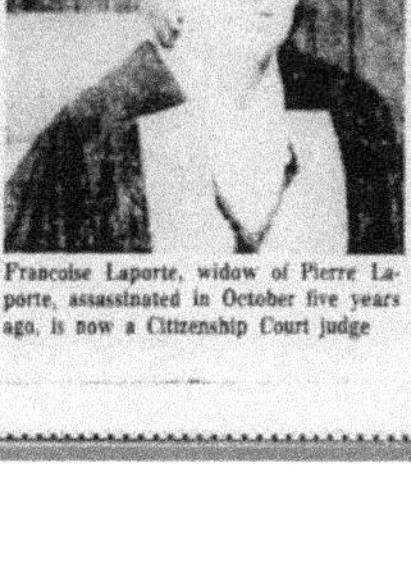

Francoise Laporte, widow of Pierre Laporte, assassinated in October five years ago, is now a Citizenship Court judge.

"REAL ESTATE BOOMS AND FINANCIAL PANICS HAVE ALWAYS BEEN CLOSE TOGETHER--FIRST THE BOOM, AND RIGHT AFTER IT THE PANIC."

(Goodwin's Weekly - Dec 16, 1905)

Real estate booms felt in east, west

By JAMES M. WOODARD

You say the age of "real estate booms" has passed into history? Look again. We are now experiencing some of the strongest booms in many decades, and at least in a few cases they are steadily picking up momentum.

Areas along the west coast have long been known for rapid growth and "hot" real estate markets But let's look eastward for a couple of current examples of booms.

Probably the hottest housing boom in the entire country is in central Florida — areas in close proximity to the new Walt Disney World, near Orlando. Fantastic increases in land values have been experienced here.

Several large-scale developments are planned for the area, including a $120 million project that will produce Florida's tallest hotel (36-story Hyatt Regency Orlando), a 6-plus acre office park, townhouse condominiums, commercial and recreation facilities. The target year for completion of the entire development is 1975.

Super-active real estate markets are noted throughout the state of Florida. Land prices have increased 10 to 30 per cent per year in most areas. A number of Gulf coast sites have doubled in value during the past two or three years. It's also interesting to note the nation's largest condominium market is Florida — the one state that can claim a third of the country's condominium starts about 40,000 units).

For an industrial real estate market boom, consider the fifth smallest state of Connecticut. Here is one of the hottest growth centers in the northwest. Over 21,000 industrial plants are now in operation, employing 40 per cent of the state's labor force.

Increasing numbers of manufacturing firms indicate a preference for Connecticut because of (1) availability of request the seller to correct the condition in your original "offer to purchase" contract.

To detect "not so obvious" defects, it will probably require an inspection by an impartial expert. You or the seller can arrange for a specialist to inspect the property and issue a "statement of condition." A few firms specialize exclusively in such inspection service, covering all basic elements of home construction and related mechanical and electrical equipment.

Q. I was interested in your column on new efforts to promote

Heating has many components

When contemplating the purchase of a warm air winter air conditioning system, be careful to give equal consideration to every element of the system, cautions

energy-conserving buildings What specific steps can be taken to save energy?

A Photo cells can be used to control some lighting Solar screens can be utilized as protection from outside heat, thus reducing energy needed to activate air conditioning units Certain electrical and mechanical equipment can be controlled by automatic timers, minimizing unneeded operation

These are a few ideas planned for a model energy-conserving building, now being designed by the General Services Administration in Washington to demonstrate needed building controls

Q. How long is a new home normally warranted against construction defects?

A. One or two years is most common. Sometimes longer, depending on policy of the builder-developer. One Canadian developer recently announced he would warrant his new homes for a period of ten years — longest warranty we've noted.

"YOU SAY THE AGE OF 'REAL ESTATE BOOMS' HAS PASSED INTO HISTORY? LOOK AGAIN."

(North Hills News Record - Jan 17, 1973)

Young left out of real estate boom

Ellen Goodman

They were talking about real estate. It is, to be frank, one of their favorite subjects.

Each of them had a story to tell. One had bought a house in 1973 for $40,000. It had just been valued at $265,000. Another had a neighbor who sold her house, tripling her money in ten years — the right ten years. A third figured carefully the inflated value of his home into his retirement plans.

They did not brag, these couples in late middle age, of having had any special prescience about a real-estate boom. They had put money down on a house in the '60s or '70s and won the jackpot of the '80s. There were no oil wells in their backyards, but the homes had made a more spectacular return than any gusher.

They simply rode the real-estate boom to a certain measure of paper profit. The houses they chose to live in were also investments to live off. They were new middle-income and house-rich. So conversations like these make them feel good or at least lucky.

But then the subject turned to their children, grown children. Could their children afford to buy the houses they had grown up in? A second set of stories poured out, more troubled than

half of new mortgages depend on second incomes.

The gap grew through the vagaries of supply and demand. Over the past 15 years, incomes fell behind inflation and houses sped ahead. Tax breaks have gone to those with mortgages, and so-called tax revolts made generational differences even more striking. In California, famed Proposition 13 froze property taxes at 1978 rates —

term dependence of "kids these days."

The "kids" of 25 and 30 have in turn become awkwardly conscious of the way that real estate has solidified the two-class structure. The have and have nots of their own age are often those who either have or have not parents with home equity. Those who will have or will not have their legacies.

I don't want to turn a real-estate

> "EACH OF THEM HAD A STORY TO TELL. ONE HAD BOUGHT A HOUSE IN 1973 FOR $40,000. IT HAD JUST BEEN VALUED AT $265,000...THEY SIMPLY RODE THE REAL ESTATE BOOM TO A CERTAIN MEASURE OF PAPER PROFIT."

(Palladium-Item - Mar 28, 1989)

Housing Prices At Peak, He Says

Washington, Feb. 13—(AP)—Housing Expediter Frank R. Creedon said today prices on new homes and building materials have reached their peak and "are beginning to level off."

Creedon emphasized in talking with reporters, however, he means only that prices "have stopped going up." He declined to forecast when they might start downward.

The expediter added that the housing program "has crystalized" sufficiently to allow a one-third cut in the agency's 1,150 employees. 30-day dismissal notices are to be issued today to 400 employes, he said.

Wise men say every day, "You can't make a boom by just selling real estate to one another." Nobody seriously thinks we can. There are many kinds of booms, and the real estate boom is only one kind. There can be, however, no other boom without a real estate boom. That is the precusor of other booms. It is the foundation boom. A town where nobody cares to buy, and nobody expects to sell real estate, may grow, but it will not boom. A town where men are willing to buy real property and are putting up their money for it every day is a boom town.

Atchison has had and is having a real estate boom. More pieces of property have been bought and sold within the last three weeks than in years before. Some of the largest transactions in real estate ever known in Kansas have occurred in this city

> "HOUSING EXPEDITER FRANK R. CREEDON SAID TODAY PRICES ON NEW HOMES AND BUILDING MATERIALS HAVE REACHED THEIR PEAK..."

(Rapid City Journal - Feb 13, 1947)

> "ATCHISON HAS HAD AND IS HAVING A REAL ESTATE BOOM."

(The Atchison Daily Champion - Apr 9, 1887)

SANTA CRUZ COUNTY SENTINEL

More first-time help
Fannie Mae offers new way to reduce mortgage insurance •
Page E2

REAL ESTATE

Sunday, January 17, 1999

E

Young buyers boost sales

Professor shows what fuels a hot real-estate market

A HOUSE WITH A
MILLION-DOLLAR
VIEW

La Selva Beach home lists for $4.5 million

"ONCE THE YOUNGEST BUYERS SIT OUT IN ANTICIPATION OF AN ECONOMIC SLUMP, THE WHOLE HOUSING PYRAMID STARTS TO CRUMBLE."

(Santa Cruz Sentinel - Jan 17, 1999)

But SIU-C professor doesn't believe it

By Ed Bean
Of The Southern Illinoisan

Clever. Well written. Intriguing. And totally irresponsible.

That is the response of Southern Illinois University-Carbondale associate professor of real estate George Karvell to "The Coming Real Estate Crash," by John Wesley English and Gray Emerson Cardiff.

"Their scenario of what would happen if we did have a crash is accurate and their history of other crashes is correct. But they make some quantum leaps from facts to conclusions.

"The historical precedents are interesting, but they fail to draw any connecting link between things such as the Florida land boom and our current situation."

There have indeed been speculative real estate booms in America's past, Karvel says, but is the current market valuation really a boom? "If the term 'boom' means that prices are not supported by underlying value, then it's not really a boom at all. Why don't they talk about the 'boom' in food prices. You don't see them advising us to wait until the price of cereal or meat comes down.

"That's because food is a basic need. Things like gold and stock have no intrinsic value and are subject to 'booms.' But housing, like food, serves a basic need. The cost of a home is supported by its utility as well as labor and materials costs."

As for a possible decline in labor costs and building materials, Karvel asks "What kind of economic situation do you think it would take for carpenters and plumbers to offer to work for substantially less money?"

Karvel admits that certain areas of the country have been subject to speculation but points out that there are other areas where the cost of housing has barely kept pace with inflation. "If it's a boom then the cost increases should be evenly distributed throughout the economy. But they haven't been. I can show you a home that sells for $85,000 in Southern Illinois that will go for $125,000 in Chicago and $250,000 in Denver but for only $45,000 in rural Georgia. And there are homes in Anna and Alto Pass that would bring substantially more if they were located in Carbondale. The disparity of prices indicates that it's not a boom at all."

And although the current high cost of borrowing money has put a damper on real estate values the demand still exists, according to Karvel. "By imposing high interest rates, the government can make it harder to exercise our demand, but the demand is there. The fact that people exists is reason for demand."

And even if the authors are right in their assertion that a sizable number of post-World War II baby-boom families have already entered the housing market, Karvel contends they fail to take into consideration social forces that are creating additional households.

"Statistics show that many people of the baby-boom years have postponed marriage and they'll be coming into the market later. An increasing divorce rate and equal credit opportunity for women has increased the number of 'non-normal' households. So even if the baby boom is declining, these factors

are going to postpone and soften its effect."

And as these households get ready to enter the housing market, they'll find that supply is still lagging far behind demand, according to Karvel. He says the number of housing starts has lagged behind estimated demand for new homes for the last decade and industry sources predict that it may take another 40 years for housing starts to catch up. "We haven't even begun to supply that demand yet, he says, "and the current crunch on credit is likely to create a situation of pent-up demand that will make the situation even worse."

Karvel sees holes in the authors' other arguments too. "They say there is an abundance of land in this country that should act to bring supply into parity with demand. There is an abundance of land — the problem is that most of it is in the wrong places. It's true you can get cheap land on the side of a mountain or in rural Illinois where you have to dig a hole for a septic tank, but that's not where most of our population wants to live. They want to live where they can have paved streets, sewers, water, schools, and libraries. And that land is expensive. Zoning and environmental restrictions will probably keep it expensive too."

Although the authors say that they think there is a trend toward removing tax breaks for homeowners, Karvel says he sees little evidence of that. "Homeowners tend to be more stable and are more active participants in the

community. It's to the government's advantage to encourage home ownership and I think it's unlikely that will change."

And is the end of inflation near?

"Even if inflation is slowed, since World War II real estate has always inflated at a rate greater than that of the general economy. I think it will continue to." He admits that the effect of deflation would be hard to predict.

Karvel does see the possibility of a downturn in real estate values "if the Federal Reserve has turned the screws too tight. We could have a situation like we had in '73 and '74 but I don't think the government would have the guts to allow to continue. People can live with inflation a lot easier than they can live with unemployment."

A crash in the real-estate market is possible, Karvel says, but only as a result of a 1930s-like depression. "Then real estate would suffer correspondingly with the rest of the economy. But if we see a real-estate crash independent of a general depression, it certainly won't be for the reasons that these guys tell us."

Nonetheless, Karvell does see changes in the nature of the market. "We're entering a period where we're having to redefine adequacy in housing. Do we really need a two-car garage, a half-acre lot and a country kitchen?"

"We're used to defining adequacy in terms of a level of prosperity that we may never see again. The world's economic pie is not getting any bigger and

as OPEC and other parts of the world demand a bigger slice, something will have to give. We'll have to have to give up something and that probably means we'll have to be satisfied with more modest housing.

"If you would have told someone in 1964 that they wouldn't be able to afford a big four-door car they would have been incredulous. What's happening with automobiles is going to happen in housing too."

> "I CAN SHOW YOU A HOME THAT SELLS FOR $85,000 IN SOUTHERN ILLINOIS THAT WILL GO FOR $125,000 IN CHICAGO AND $250,000 IN DENVER BUT FOR ONLY $45,000 IN RURAL GEORGIA. THE DISPARITY OF PRICES INDICATES THAT ITS NOT A BOOM AT ALL."
>
> *(Southern Illinoisan – Jan 25, 1979)*

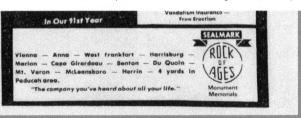

Expert recounts explorer Lewis' botany interests

Quiz requires a good memory

Brucellosis can be eradicated, vet says

should be careful, forest official says

"BOZEMAN HOUSE PRICES PEAK"

(The Billings Gazette - Jun 5, 1995)

Bozeman housing prices peak

Salmon stolen from hatchery

Lower cattle prices threaten ranchers

TV SPECIAL

BILLY GRAHAM

"Are You
Ready for
Christ's Return?"

TONIGHT 7:00 KULR/8

Watch Tuesday, June 6 • 8:00 PM • KULR/8
"Why the Cross?"

IS A REAL ESTATE BOOM COMING?

BABSON CONTINUES HIS DISCUSSION OF INFLATION

ROGER BABSON

Babson Park, Mass., February 12. Everyone is asking what will happen to business, employment, agriculture, the railroads and other affairs after World War II. Even an interest is developing in the long-forgotten stock market. I have my opinions about all these things; but of necessity they must be subject to change in the light of new conditions. Hence, we will not now discuss them.

Real Estate Booms Once a Generation

Of one thing I am certain,—that is we are headed for a much more active real estate market. I will not now forecast a real estate boom— but such may occur. Moreover, I haven't any land to sell! The only bit of land that I own personally is that upon which my Wellesley, Massachusetts, home is located.

Statistics, however, show that a real estate boom comes once every generation. Biologists figure a generation at twenty-one years or more. Thus, the children of every generation must have a fling at real estate themselves. They refuse to listen to their parents' advice. This may even apply to Florida, which had a boom in 1924-1926. This means that those who are now thirty years of age were only twelve when the Florida boom was on—that is, they don't remember it. They are the ones to start another land boom.

Money Cannot Be Destroyed

There is some real logic for a land boom after World War II. I have in mind the tremendous and unlimited supply of bank deposits, cashable goverment bonds and pocketbook currency which will be floating about this country. The government spends $250,000 for a bomber which is destroyed, or $2,-500,000 for a ship which is sunk; but the money is neither destroyed nor sunk. It remains in banks, bonds or stockings, although its purchasing power may be destroyed.

Someday this money will be spent for something. It will continue to circulate for a long time. During the process, much of it will go into real estate. Buying bonds and paying taxes will postpone inflation; but not prevent it. The money which we pay into the government for bonds or taxes is immediately paid out to farmers, wage workers and others. Sooner or later they are going to buy something with it before its purchasing power declines.

Homes Are Good Investments

Readers should remember that inflation does ... ... Owing to the ... ber, aluminu... raw materials ... able after the sible these w... With ten mill... there surely w... vances. Owing ... government b... very sharp ... manufacturers ... ness. This ma... ting.

Hence, what will these incomprehensible billions of dollars go into? What will go up in price due to increased buying? In what will people speculate to satisfy their unquenchable instincts? In what will the thrifty invest when they get tired of holding depreciating currency? My answer is, "Either land or stocks." Certainly, a small well-located modern home with enough land for a garden is a good investment.

How Booms Are Caused

Of course, much of this money will go into automobiles, refrigerators, television radios and furniture of all kinds. Houses will be repaired and repainted. New clothes will be bought and a thousand other channels of trade come to life for awhile. All of these things are, however, mere chicken feed to what can be spent for land and stocks when a boom is on. Also remember that even then the money is not destroyed! The chap yo... buy the land or stocks from ha... your money and will use it to buy some more land or stocks.

A depression is caused by every one wanting to sell. A boom ... caused by everyone wanting to buy. Booms collapse when too man... people who have borrowed mone... are called upon to pay their loans. This, they cannot do without selling more property. The result is ... general decline in values which means more loans are called and so things go from bad to worse. Finally, prices get so low that they look ridiculous and buyers come into the market and the depression is over.

Times Are Different Today

Of course, some day we shall have another depression and it will be a sad one.— probably worse tha... the last. In the meantime, however, there is sure to be a boom i... real estate and—if the S.E.C. does not kill it—also a boom in stocks. Why am I saying there is time before then for a real estate boom? Here is my answer. Today the

"STATISTICS HOWEVER SHOW THAT A REAL ESTATE BOOM COMES ONCE EVERY GENERATION."

(The Daily Republican - Feb 12, 1943)

'Feelings' trigger real estate booms

NEW HAVEN, Conn. (AP) — A survey of home buyers in four U.S. cities has led two economists to conclude that shifting perceptions of market conditions, and not simply changing economic variables, cause real estate booms.

While home buyers cited economic reasons for purchasing a house at a particular time, the researchers say they believe the people were ac-

their reach unless they buy immediately, or when they think they can make a great deal of money by investing right away, Shiller said.

But he said there is no conclusive evidence as to what triggers the change in perceptions that leads to panic buying and higher prices. Most studies, he said, have looked only at economic variables to attempt to explain real estate booms

In San Francisco, prices increased more than 10%, from May to June 1988, while in Anaheim they rose more than 4% during the same time period.

In Boston, considered to be representative of the Northeast corridor in its post-boom real estate market, prices that had doubled from 1984 to 1987 have been slipping.

e, the average price of a house has annually in the past five years, > $71,500.

e surveyed claimed that changes in prompted their buying decisions st rates were responsible for the ity's real estate markets. said those explanations did not cause each area was actually expe erent real estate market.

continued on page 3

> ## "WHILE HOMEBUYERS CITED ECONOMIC REASONS FOR PURCHASING A HOUSE AT A PARTICULAR TIME, THE RESEARCHERS SAY THEY BELIEVE THE PEOPLE WERE ACTUALLY RESPONDING TO THE EMOTIONAL ASSESS-MENTS OF PROPERTY VALUES."

(The Post-Crescent – Nov 8, 1988)

Homes...

Continued from page 1

"Interest rates were cited as being responsible for dramatic pr--- ---creases on the West Coast, d on the East Coast, and stable in the middle regions," he sa

Home buyers in San Francis Anaheim also cited a healthy r economy and the desirability ing in their cities as explanati the dramatic increases in h costs.

The home buyers were "ret: into cliches and images for e: tions rather than citing any c evidence," Shiller said.

"The responses leave the strong impression that people look at changes in the prices of houses to form their opinions and then search for a logic to explain or reinforce their beliefs."

Little research has been done about these occurrences and there is even less agreement among economists about the underlying causes of dramatic price movements, he said.

> ## "THE RESPONSES LEAVE THE STRONG IMPRESSION THAT PEOPLE LOOK AT CHANGES IN THE PRICES OF HOUSES TO FORM THEIR OPINIONS AND THEN SEARCH FOR A LOGIC TO EXPLAIN OR REINFORCE THEIR BELIEFS."

(The Post-Crescent – Nov 8, 1988)

Money matters

Tulare Advance-Register

14B

Weekend, September 20-21 2003

Newsroom: 688-0521
www.TulareAdvanceRegister.com

PAT DANIELS
YOUR MONEY

Allocate as you invest

As many investors have learned, building wealth while preserving principal is not about riding the hot sectors or even picking the "best" investments.

It's about investing regularly over the long term with a diversified portfolio. Your portfolio's asset allocation — the mix of investments you choose — is key to achieving diversity, maximizing returns and managing risk, even more than your choice of actual investments. Whether you dream of retiring in style, sending your children to the university of their choice or starting your own business, now you allocate your assets will be critical to achieving your goals.

A diversified portfolio begins with three main asset classes: stocks, bonds and cash. Each of these performs differently in different situations. They also offer different levels of risk and potential return. Your investments should reflect your age, your individual needs and goals, and the overall economy.

► **Stocks.** Stocks represent shares of ownership in the companies that issue them. These are your best shot at long-term growth (rather than short-term income) and may represent the majority of your portfolio, depending on your time horizon. Though more risky than bonds or cash, stocks have produced higher average annual returns over time and offer the best long-term potential hedge against inflation. According to Ibbotson Associates, a respected financial services consulting firm, there has been no 15-year or longer period when stocks, as represented by the S&P 500 index, didn't seem a gain. Fifty-four of the past 76 years have seen the stock market gain money.

It's also important to diversify your stock holdings. Growth and value stocks should be well-represented in your portfolio, with exposure to large-, mid- and small-caps, as well as international and sector funds, depending on your risk factor.

► **Bonds.** Bonds are essentially a type of debt issued by corporations and governments when they borrow money. In repayment for the loan, bond issuers promise to pay interest to the bondholder for the life of the bond. At maturity, the bond is retired and the principal amount repaid. A rise in interest rates generally results in a decline in the value of a bond. Bond prices tend to fluctuate less than stocks.

► **Cash.** Not only the green stuff that lines your pocket, "cash" also includes taxable and tax-free money market funds, CDs and treasury bills. These are among the lowest-risk investments, but they dangerously lower potential returns compared to stocks and bonds, with CDs and treasury bills fluctuating less than money markets.

You can access general online asset allocation tools through investment Web sites, but you might also wish to seek the advice of a financial adviser.

Together with your advisor, you should examine your portfolio frequently to ensure that your allocation is not shifting significantly because of movements in the market or changes in your own personal situation.

This article does not constitute tax or legal advice. Consult an adviser before making any tax or legally related decisions. This article is for general information only and is not an offer or solicitation to sell or buy any securities or commodities. Any particular investment should be analyzed based on its terms and risks.

Patricia A. Daniels is an investment broker in Visalia. Her column runs monthly in the Money Matters section. Write her via the Visalia Times-Delta, P.O. Box 31, Visalia, CA 93278.

Housing prices peak out

The median home price, which is the sales midpoint, has dropped 2.2 percent since the last quarter of 2002, and evidence is growing that the housing market has peaked. Industry forecasters expect home price growth to continue dropping.

SOURCE: National Association of Realtors

By Thomas A. Fogarty
Gannett News Service

HOME PRICE$

KNOW WHICH WAY THE WIND BLOWS

Economists have been predicting wrongly for more than a year that the surge in home prices is about to moderate. The recent run-up in mortgage interest rates now gives everyone a reason to believe them.

In a slowing market, home shoppers are at higher risk of buying at the top, taking on excessive monthly payments, and setting up for financial disaster when they go to sell for less than they paid.

Buyers have no surefire way to protect against paying a price today that will leave them kicking themselves in a year or two. But in home buying, knowledge is power. And experts say a well-informed buyer can minimize the chance of diving into a frenzied market just ahead of a big crash.

Evidence is growing that the housing market nationally has peaked. The average interest rate on a 30-year fixed-rate mortgage is up by more than a full percentage point since June, and now stands at 6.44 percent. As a result, applications for purchase mortgages have softened. Industry forecasters generally agree that by the end of the year, the rate of sales will decline from its record, and home price growth, which has been running at 7 percent plus, will slow by half.

"In the near future, price increases will stall, even decline, in some cities," economists Robert Shiller of Yale University and Karl Case of Wellesley College concluded in a report this week to the Brookings Institution, a Washington, D.C., think tank. Most at risk, they say, are cities where home prices "have been freely, notably cities on both coasts, and especially those cities that have weakening economies."

So if your boss tells you that

Inside

Interest-only mortgages are gaining in popularity.**15B**

you're being transferred to sub-urban New York City — which has been among the hottest markets in the country — what do you do to reduce the possibility of overpaying for a house?

Choosing an agent

All real estate commissions come from the seller's proceeds when the sale is closed. So there's no good financial reason for a buyer not to sign on with an agent to guide the home search.

When it comes to making an offer on a house, a good agent should have two things you don't: The most current data from recent sales of comparable property through Realtor-controlled multiple listing services, and local knowledge. By

going to open houses every day a good agent develops a sense when a hot neighborhood is cooling.

Chris Heagarty, general manager for eRealty in Austin, says buyers get better service when they work with a single agent rather than contacting different agents for each property on their shopping list.

A written agreement between shopper and agent clarifies services that will be provided, she says.

But be aware of your agent's potential conflicts. The same real estate brokerage may be representing both you and the seller. The brokerage's first allegiance is to the seller, who, after all, is paying everybody's commission. That can compromise the advice you get on deciding how much to bid. Such built-in conflicts have given rise to realty firms that take no property listings and instead represent buyers only. They're worth a look.

If you're dealing with an agent whose brokerage deals on both sides of the transaction, be careful. At the time you make an offer to buy, you're depending mainly on the integrity of your agent to make sure your interests are protected.

Matures can get particularly difficult if you decide to make an offer on a house that your own agent has listed.

When that happens, Heagarty, whose firm represents both buyers and sellers, advises that an outside agent be brought into the deal. By having an outsider write and present your offer, your agent's conflict is minimized.

Find out about local markets

In mid-2002, the median price for homes in Bergen and Passaic counties in New Jersey was growing at 24.7 percent annually. By mid-2003, annual price growth had slowed to 7.1 percent. It's a handy thing to know for a buyer coming into that suburban New York market. But that which the custodian of such information?

In this case, it's the National Association of Realtors, one of three key trackers of local market price trends. Here's what they tell you about local prices and how to find them on the Internet:

► **NAR.** NAR reports quarterly on changes in median prices — the sales midpoint — for more than 100 metro areas. The NAR data have weaknesses. Several big cities — Detroit and Cleveland, for example — don't report. And sometimes median prices shift because of the changing mix in the types of homes that are selling, not because prices are being bid up or down. Find the information at Realtor.org. Click "research," then "existing-home sales."

See Home/15B

Workers retool in tough times

By Steve Rhode
and Mike Kidwell
Gannett News Service

Question: I lost my $18,000-a-year job and was only able to find a job that pays $9 an hour. Now that job is being eliminated. I guess my next job will eat up my salary in half again and I'll make $4 an hour. On top of all that, I'm 55 and I have $20,000 in debt. Why is it so hard to start over?

Answer: Without a doubt, our national economy is changing. Many jobs in good paying fields are being completely eliminated. Some companies are even exporting or outsourcing professional and executive jobs.

These changes are driven by many factors, but one is a thirst from Wall Street and stockholders that practically requires companies to be more and more profitable every year. Running a business has many things in common with managing the finances of a household. When businesses face tough competition in difficult economic times, they are faced with two choices: lower their costs or increase sales.

It wasn't all that long ago when the computer field was the hot place to be and now even jobs in that industry are being shed. Today there are many jobs open for hair stylists and morticians than there are people to fill them. Next, we're not suggesting that you go into either of those careers, but you can't sit still. Today is the day to reinvent yourself.

As far as the debt goes, without a reliable process you shouldn't make any promises to pay that you really can't keep. If you've got collectors calling, be honest about your situation, but don't make promises to pay a certain amount that you will not be able to make consistently until the debt is satisfied. That will only make things worse.

Question: I just got the credit card bill for all of my kids' back-to-school shopping. I had no idea, but we spent $1,320. That's for three kids. I can't afford it!

Answer: We're surprised that you didn't spend more. Our national survey found that the average family planned to spend about $1,500 this year and that was down 27 percent from 2002.

Back-to-school shopping is part of the triffecta of debt. Too, like most Americans, probably spend at three key times — in-lay holidays, summer vacations and back to school. Your situation is a symptom of a bigger issue. It's not like you were not prepared for and comfortable with some amount of back-to-school shopping. Let's say you spent $400 more than you planned. If $400 throws you into a tailspin, then you are living too close to financial disaster. Use this as a warning sign and let's come up with a plan that will allow you to be safe and, more importantly, happy.

Send questions to Myvesting Questions, P.O. Box 8587, Gaithersburg, Md. 20898-8587 or e-mail questions@myvesta.org.

Families ca...

The Associated P...
NEW YORK —...
their mother's...
Lee Yurban and...
a big fight and st...
each other.

Yurdam and...
decided they w...
wood nightstand...
er's house, a pa...
belonged to thei...

"There were te...
we could have been arguing about," said Yurdam, 51, of Sherman Oaks. "But we were both caught up in the emotionalism after my mother died, and that caused things to happen that I would never have dreamed of."

More families have stories of fights that erupted after a loved one's death, pitting brother against

sister, families... comrade — before death, whether verbally or in writing — can avoid such family-wrenching spats.

"It really helps if the person talks to the kids and ask questions like, 'Do we have anything you really want?'" said attorney Denis Clifford, author of the book "Estate Planning Basics." "Then they can...

...ended several weeks later," after Wilder's teenage son climbed the table with a strong household dislodge and destroyed the flower...

"Gems, I called me," Yurdam remembers. "She was laughing and told me what he had done. Soon we were both laughing, then crying." And talking again.

"The lesson learned for us was, "beloved, family comes first — just like my mother always said," Yurdam said.

Lee Kotyn, a Montreal lawyer who specializes in wills and estates, said more people intuitively believe disputes only happen in rich families.

"People don't just fight over money, they fight over memories."

...he said. "People think, 'I'm just a millionaire so why should I worry?' Then their heirs end up fighting over a watch."

Kotyn, with partner Barry Fish, wrote "The Family Fight — Planning to Avoid It," it gives families ways to work things out through good record keeping, gifts, charity, wills and a power of attorney.

CPSIA information can be obtained
at www.ICGtesting.com
Printed in the USA
FSHW011536080719